# Growing in the Faith

# A Simple Guide to Bible and Christian Doctrine

Author – Eld Joel Latimore Jr.

**Growing in the Faith**

A Simple Guide to Bible and Christian Doctrine

Written by Eld Joel Latimore Jr.

© 2026 Eld Joel Latimore Jr.

Latimore Publishing

ISBN (paperback): 979-8-218-88610-3

All rights reserved. No part of this book may be reproduced, stored in a retrieval system, or transmitted in any form or by any means—electronic, mechanical, photocopying, recording, or otherwise—without the prior written permission of the publisher, except for brief quotations used in reviews or scholarly works.

Scripture quotations are taken from the King James Version (KJV) of the Bible, unless otherwise noted.

**EPIGRAPH**

*But grow in grace, and in the knowledge of our Lord and Saviour Jesus Christ.*

*— 2 Peter 3:18*

# TABLE OF CONTENTS

- Dedication

- Preface

- Introduction                **Pg 1**

Ch 1 Understanding the Bible…      **Pg 4**

Ch 2 How We Got the Bible…       **Pg 35**

Ch 3 The First Principles …         **Pg 61**

Ch 4 Who God Is …              **Pg 107**

| | |
|---|---|
| Ch 5  Who Jesus Is … | **Pg 135** |
| Ch 6  The Holy Ghost … | **Pg 160** |
| Ch 7  Holy Living … | **Pg 185** |
| Ch 8  Worship & Prayer … | **Pg 210** |
| Ch 9  The Church … | **Pg 236** |
| Ch 10 Spiritual Growth & Maturity … | **Pg 262** |
| Ch 11 Witnessing & Winning Souls … | **Pg 292** |
| Ch 12 Serving Others … | **Pg 317** |

Ch 13  How to Study Your Bible					**Pg 345**

Ch 14 Reading the Bible in One Year			**Pg 371**

- Conclusion								**Pg 389**

- Acknowledgment							**Pg 392**

- About the Author							**Pg 395**

# DEDICATION

This book is dedicated to every believer—new in the faith or seasoned in years—who desires a clearer understanding of God's Word and the foundational truths of the Christian life.

Many have walked with the Lord faithfully, yet were never taught the basic doctrines that strengthen spiritual growth. Others are just beginning their journey and are eager to learn the essentials of living for Christ.

Wherever you are on your spiritual path, may this simple guide help you grow in wisdom, confidence, and stability. May it fill in the gaps, answer long-held questions, and provide clarity where there has been uncertainty.

And may the Holy Spirit illuminate every truth, deepen your understanding, and lead you into a richer, stronger, more joyful walk with the Lord Jesus Christ.

To all who desire to **grow in the faith**—this book is lovingly dedicated to you.

# PREFACE

**Growing in the Faith** was written to help believers build a strong and steady foundation in their walk with God. In every church, there are precious saints—both new and seasoned—who love the Lord deeply but have never been taught the basic truths of the Bible. Many do not know how the Scriptures are arranged, how many books the Bible contains, who wrote them, or how the major themes of the Bible fit together.

Others have served faithfully for years, yet still feel unsure when it comes to understanding the foundational doctrines of the Christian faith.

This book was created to meet that need with simplicity, clarity, and compassion.

In these pages, you will find a gentle, step-by-step guide to the essential teachings of Scripture. You will learn not only what Christians believe, but why we, as **the Church Of God In Christ,** believe it—and how those truths shape our daily lives.

The goal is not to overwhelm you with information, but to walk with you as a pastor would, explaining the things many believers were never taught but always needed to know.

Here, we will explore both the structure of the Bible and the basic doctrines that support a healthy spiritual life. Whether you are taking your first steps as a new believer or strengthening foundations that were never fully laid, this study is designed to help you grow in understanding, confidence, and spiritual maturity.

My prayer is that as you read, the Holy Spirit will open your understanding and illuminate the truth of God's Word. May this book bring clarity where there has been confusion, stability where there has been uncertainty, and joy where there has been hesitation.

Welcome to your journey of Growing in the Faith.

May the Lord bless you richly as you build a firm foundation in His Word.

— **Eld Joel Latimore Jr.**

# INTRODUCTION

In every church, there are precious believers who love God sincerely yet struggle to understand the basics of the Bible. Some do not know how many books are in the Bible, how the Scriptures are arranged, or who wrote the different books.

Others have been saved for years but were never taught the foundational doctrines that make the Christian life strong, stable, and joyful. And new believers often feel overwhelmed because they are starting without a clear guide to help them understand God's Word.

This book was written to meet that need.

**Growing in the Faith** is a simple guide designed to help believers—both new and seasoned—gain a basic, confident understanding of the Scriptures and the essential doctrines of Christianity.

It is not meant to be complicated. It is meant to walk with you step by step, answering questions that many are embarrassed to ask, and explaining truths that every Christian should know.

Here, you will learn how the Bible is structured, how many books it contains, who wrote them, and why they matter. You will discover the major teachings of the faith: salvation, prayer, the Holy Ghost, sanctification, Christian living, and more. These truths are not only for scholars; they are for everyday believers who desire to know God better and grow stronger in their walk with Him.

My prayer is that as you read, the Holy Spirit will open your understanding and give you clarity, confidence, and joy in the Word of God.

No matter where you begin—whether you are a new believer or someone who has been in the church for many years—this book will help you build a foundation that will bless your life for years to come.

May you grow in grace, in knowledge, and in the peace that comes from understanding God's truth.

Welcome to your journey of **Growing in the Faith.**

# CHAPTER 1 — UNDERSTANDING THE BIBLE: ITS BOOKS, STRUCTURE, AND WHY WE TRUST IT

The Bible is the foundation of the Christian faith. Everything we believe—about God, salvation, holiness, prayer, the Holy Ghost, and Christian living—comes from the Scriptures. Yet many faithful believers, both new and seasoned, have never been taught how the Bible is put together, how many books it contains, who wrote them, or how the major parts of the Bible fit into one unified story.

This chapter is written to help you understand the Bible in a simple, clear, and welcoming way.

When you understand how the Bible is organized, you will read it with more confidence, study it with more clarity, and apply it with greater boldness. The more you know about God's Word, the stronger your walk with God becomes.

## What Is the Bible?

The Bible is the holy, inspired, and written Word of God. It is not like any other book. It speaks with divine authority, reveals God's plan of salvation, and teaches us how to live a life that pleases Him.

The Bible tells us about God, humanity, sin, righteousness, redemption, judgment, and eternal life. It reveals the heart of God and His will for His people.

**Scripture says:**

*"All scripture is given by inspiration of God, and is profitable for doctrine, for reproof, for correction, for instruction in righteousness."*

**— 2 Timothy 3:16**

The phrase *"inspiration of God"* means God-breathed. Though written by many human authors, the words came from God Himself. The Holy Ghost guided the writers so that what they wrote was exactly what God wanted us to receive.

**The Bible is divided into two major sections:**

1. The Old Testament — **39 books**

2. The New Testament — **27 books**

Together, they make **66 books,** forming one unified message about God's love, holiness, and redemption through Jesus Christ.

**How Many Books Are in the Bible?**

There are **66 books** in the Bible:

- **39 books** in the Old Testament
- **27 books** in the New Testament

These books were written over a period of about **1,500 years,** by more than **40 different authors,** in **three different languages,** on **three different continents.** Yet they all tell one story—the story of God's plan to redeem mankind.

This unity is one of the strongest reasons we trust the Bible. No human being could create such a consistent message across centuries. Only the Holy Ghost could produce a book like this.

## How the Old Testament Is Organized

The Old Testament is divided into five major categories, each with a specific purpose. Understanding these categories helps you see how God was working through Israel and preparing the world for the coming of Jesus.

**1. The first five books of the Bible are called the Law of Moses (The Pentateuch) — 5 Books**

1. Genesis

2. Exodus

3. Leviticus

4. Numbers

5. Deuteronomy

These books reveal God as Creator, the beginning of Israel, the giving of the Law, and God's covenant with His people.

## 2. Old Testament History — 12 Books

6. Joshua

7. Judges

8. Ruth

9. 1 Samuel

10. 2 Samuel

11. 1 Kings

12. 2 Kings

13. 1 Chronicles

14. 2 Chronicles

15. Ezra

16. Nehemiah

17. Esther

These books record Israel's journey—their victories, failures, kings, judges, wars, exile, and restoration. They teach us how God leads, corrects, and restores His people.

## 3. Poetry and Wisdom — 5 Books

18. Job

19. Psalms

20. Proverbs

21. Ecclesiastes

22. Song of Solomon

These books express worship, life's questions, suffering, praise, wisdom, and the beauty of God's relationship with His people.

## 4. The Major Prophets — 5 Books

23. Isaiah

24. Jeremiah

25. Lamentations

26. Ezekiel

27. Daniel

**"Major"** refers to the length of the books—not their importance. These prophets warned Israel, foretold the coming of Christ, and revealed God's plans for the nations.

## 5. The Minor Prophets — 12 Books

28. Hosea

29. Joel

30. Amos

31. Obadiah

32. Jonah

33. Micah

34. Nahum

35. Habakkuk

36. Zephaniah

37. Haggai

38. Zechariah

39. Malachi

These twelve books are shorter, but they contain powerful messages of warning, repentance, judgment, and hope.

## How the New Testament Is Organized

The New Testament tells us about Jesus Christ, the birth of the church, Christian doctrine, and the future hope of believers.

It is divided into four main categories.

**1. The Gospels — 4 Books**

These books tell the story of Jesus—His birth, ministry, miracles, teachings, death, and resurrection.

1. Matthew

2. Mark

3. Luke

4. John

The Gospels are the foundation of the Christian message. Everything begins with Jesus.

## 2. New Testament History — 1 Book

**Acts of the Apostles or the Acts of the Holy Ghost**

This book describes the coming of the Holy Ghost, the birth of the church, the ministry of the apostles, and the spread of the gospel.

## 3. The Epistles (Letters) — 21 Books

These letters teach Christian doctrine and daily living.

## Paul's Epistles — 13 Books

1. Romans
2. 1 Corinthians
3. 2 Corinthians
4. Galatians
5. Ephesians
6. Philippians
7. Colossians
8. 1 Thessalonians
9. 2 Thessalonians
10. 1 Timothy

11. 2 Timothy

12. Titus

13. Philemon

**General Epistles — 8 Books**

1. Hebrews

2. James

3. 1 Peter

4. 2 Peter

5. 1 John

6. 2 John

7. 3 John

8. Jude

These books give instructions about faith, holiness, spiritual growth, leadership, prayer, and the life of the church.

## 4. New Testament Prophecy — 1 Book

**Revelation**

This book reveals Jesus Christ as the victorious King and describes God's plan for the end times, the final judgment, and the eternal kingdom.

# Why We Trust the Bible (Beginner Apologetics)

Christians trust the Bible because it is:

## 1. Inspired by God

*All scripture is given by inspiration of God...*

**— 2 Timothy 3:16**

## 2. Historically accurate

Archaeology confirms people, places, and events recorded in Scripture.

## 3. Prophetically reliable

Hundreds of prophecies about Jesus were fulfilled exactly as written.

## 4. Preserved through centuries

The Bible has more manuscripts than any ancient book, proving its accuracy.

## 5. Unified in its message

Despite **40+ authors** over **1,500 years,** the Bible tells one story—Jesus Christ.

No other book in history has this kind of unity, accuracy, and divine power.

## HISTORICAL NOTE: CHURCH OF GOD IN CHRIST (COGIC) AND THE WORD OF GOD

**Bishop Charles Harrison Mason (1866–1961),** founder of the Church Of God In Christ, built this great holiness church upon the unshakable foundation of God's Word.

From the earliest days of the COGIC church, Bishop Mason emphasized that every believer—young and old—must know, love, and obey the Scriptures.

He believed the Bible to be the inspired, infallible Word of God and insisted that holiness, doctrine, and Christian living must flow from Scripture alone.

His reverence for the Word shaped the identity of COGIC and continues to influence our teaching, worship, and spiritual growth today.

This book follows in that same tradition, helping believers understand the Bible clearly and grow stronger in the faith.

## CLOSING CHARGE

Now that you have learned how the Bible is organized—its books, categories, and the beautiful way God has woven His truth through Scripture—I challenge you to take the next step in your spiritual journey: commit yourself to becoming a student of the Word.

Do not be intimidated by the size of the Bible or discouraged by what you do not yet know. Every believer, whether young or old, new in the faith or seasoned in the church, begins by taking one step at a time.

As you grow in your understanding of how the Bible is structured, you will begin to read it with confidence, study it with purpose, and apply it with joy.

Let the Holy Ghost guide your learning. Open your Bible daily. Ask God for understanding. And remember that the same Spirit who inspired the Scriptures lives inside of you to help you grow in truth.

You are on a path of spiritual strength and stability. Keep walking. Keep learning. Keep growing in the faith.

# REFLECTIVE SUMMARY

In this chapter, you explored the foundation of the Bible—its purpose, its structure, and why believers trust it as the inspired Word of God. You learned that:

The Bible contains **66 books,** written by more than **40 authors,** yet united by one message.

The Old Testament has **39 books** grouped into five major categories, beginning with the Law of Moses.

The New Testament has **27 books** grouped into four major categories, centered on the life of Jesus and the birth of the Church.

Christians trust the Bible because it is inspired, historically accurate, prophetically reliable, unified in message, and preserved by God.

**Bishop C. H. Mason,** founder of the Church Of God In Christ (COGIC), built our church's foundation on the authority of Scripture.

Understanding these basics strengthens your faith, deepens your confidence in God's Word, and prepares you for the journey ahead.

# REFLECTIVE QUESTIONS

1. Which section of the Bible **(Law, History, Poetry, Prophets, Gospels, Epistles, etc.)** do you feel most familiar with, and which section do you want to understand better?

2. Why is it important for believers—both new and seasoned—to understand how the Bible is structured?

3. How does knowing the unity and reliability of Scripture strengthen your personal faith in God?

4. What stood out to you most about the Old Testament and New Testament categories?

5. How can you begin building a more consistent habit of reading and studying the Bible each day?

## CLOSING PRAYER

Father, I thank You for giving me the gift of Your holy Word. Thank You for opening my understanding and helping me see how the Scriptures are beautifully organized and divinely inspired.

As I continue to learn, teach me to love Your Word, to trust Your truth, and to rely on the Holy Ghost for guidance. Strengthen my desire to study, to grow, and to walk faithfully in what You reveal.

**In Jesus' Name, Amen.**

## CHAPTER 2 - HOW WE GOT THE BIBLE: INSPIRATION, PRESERVATION, AND WHY THE WORD OF GOD CAN BE TRUSTED

Many believers accept the Bible as the Word of God but have never been taught how we received the Scriptures or why we can trust the Bible with confidence.

Understanding where the Bible came from, how it was preserved, and why Christians believe it is the authoritative Word of God will strengthen your faith and help you stand firm in a world filled with doubts, opinions, and false teachings.

This chapter will walk you through the simple yet powerful truth of how God gave us His Word—so that even new believers and senior saints can clearly understand the miracle of the Bible's existence.

## The Bible Did Not Come From Man—It Came From God

The Bible is not a book of human ideas, personal opinions, or spiritual guesses. It is the revelation of God Himself. The Scriptures repeatedly declare that God—through the Holy Ghost—moved upon men to write His words.

*"Knowing this first, that no prophecy of the scripture is of any private interpretation. For the prophecy came not in old time by the will of man: but holy men of God spake as they were moved by the Holy Ghost."*

**— 2 Peter 1:20–21**

Scripture is not man reaching up to God—it is God reaching down to man.

God used *the personalities, writing styles*, and *experiences of the authors*, but every word was guided and inspired by the Holy Ghost. This is what we call:

**Divine Inspiration**

**Inspiration** means God-breathed.

It means the Bible carries *the breath, power,* and *authority* of God Himself.

*"All scripture is given by inspiration of God..."*

**— 2 Timothy 3:16**

When you read the Bible, you are not just reading history.

You are not reading myths or religious traditions.

You are reading the voice of God speaking through chosen vessels.

## How God Preserved His Word

Not only did God give His Word—He protected it.

For thousands of years, rulers, empires, and enemies tried to destroy the Scriptures. But God preserved **His Word through:**

- faithful scribes

- dedicated prophets

- early church leaders

- countless believers who protected the manuscripts

Today, we possess thousands of ancient copies of biblical manuscripts—more than any other ancient document in the world. This overwhelming evidence proves:

**\*\*The Bible has not been lost.**

The Bible has not been corrupted.

The Bible has been preserved. \*\*

**Jesus Himself declared:**

*"Heaven and earth shall pass away, but my words shall not pass away."* — **Matthew 24:35**

God protects His Word because God speaks through His Word.

## The Bible We Have Today Is Reliable and Accurate

Some ask, "How do we know the Bible is accurate if it was copied so many times?"

**The answer is simple:**

**God preserved His Word with remarkable accuracy.**

**Compared to other ancient writings:**

- Homer's Iliad has fewer than **2,000 ancient copies.**

- Aristotle's writings have fewer than **50 copies.**

- BUT the New Testament alone has over **5,800 Greek manuscripts** and thousands more in other languages.

With so many copies, scholars can compare them and confirm their accuracy.

The result: the Bible is over **99% textually pure.**

No other ancient document comes close.

This is why Christians confidently **say:**

**The Bible you read today is the same Bible God inspired long ago.**

## Why the Early Church Trusted These Books

The early church did not randomly choose which books belonged in the Bible. They recognized the books that were:

- written by apostles or close companions

- consistent with the teachings of Jesus

- widely accepted by early believers

- proven to be inspired

- faithful to the doctrine delivered to the saints

The church did not give the books authority—

God gave the books authority, and the church recognized what God had already established.

**This process gave us:**

The **39 books** of the Old Testament

The **27 books** of the New Testament

These **66 books** form the complete, trustworthy Bible we use today.

## The Bible Is God's Message to Humanity

Why did God give us the Bible?

Because He wanted us to know Him—not through guesswork, but through truth.

**The Scriptures reveal:**

- God's character

- God's commandments

- God's promises

- God's plan of salvation

- God's standards of holiness

- God's will for our lives

Without the Bible, we would not know who God is or how to please Him.

**David wrote:**

*"Thy word is a lamp unto my feet, and a light unto my path."*
— **Psalm 119:105**

God's Word gives light, direction, correction, and hope.

## The Role of the Holy Ghost in Understanding Scripture

The Bible is spiritually understood.

This means that even though anyone can read it, only the Holy Ghost can help us understand it.

**Jesus said:**

*But the Comforter, which is the Holy Ghost... he shall teach you all things.*

**— John 14:26**

This is why some people read the Bible for years and never grow— they are depending on intellect instead of the Spirit.

But when the Holy Ghost becomes your Teacher:

- the Scriptures come alive

- your understanding grows

- confusion disappears

- truth becomes clear

- conviction becomes strong

- and your faith is built up

Every believer needs both **the Word of God** and **the Spirit of God** to grow.

# HISTORICAL NOTE: BISHOP C. H. MASON AND THE BIBLE

Bishop Charles Harrison Mason, founder of the Church Of God In Christ (COGIC), believed in the complete inspiration and authority of Scripture. He taught that the Holy Ghost not only inspired the Bible but illuminates it for every believer.

Bishop Mason insisted that *holiness, doctrine,* and *church life* must be grounded in the Word of God—not opinions, customs, or traditions. His deep reverence for Scripture laid the foundation for our church and continues to guide COGIC believers in faith and practice.

**His example reminds us:**

A holiness church must be a Bible-believing church.

## The Bible Is Our Final Authority

In the Church Of God In Christ, **we preach:**

**"The Bible is right."**

It is our final voice of authority—not feelings, not culture, not society, and not human ideas.

**The Bible is:**

- the foundation of truth

- the standard of righteousness

- the measure of doctrine

- the source of wisdom

- the guide for holy living

Every believer must build their life—not on emotion—but on the Word of God.

## CLOSING CHARGE

Now that you understand how we received the Bible—by divine inspiration and through God's faithful preservation—I challenge you to deepen your trust in the Word of God.

The Scriptures you read are not accidental, corrupted, or uncertain. They are the very words God intended for you to have. Stand firmly on the truth that God has spoken, God has preserved His Word, and God continues to speak to your heart through Scripture.

Approach your Bible with reverence. Open it daily with expectation. Ask the Holy Ghost to illuminate the text and guide your understanding.

As you grow in confidence that the Bible is the true and trustworthy Word of God, your walk with Christ will become stronger, your faith will become deeper, and your spiritual foundation will become unshakable.

# REFLECTIVE SUMMARY

In this chapter, you learned that the Bible did not come from human imagination but from the inspiration of the Holy Ghost. You discovered that:

- Holy men wrote as the Spirit moved upon them.

- God preserved His Word through centuries with remarkable accuracy.

- The Bible has more manuscript evidence than any ancient document.

- The early church recognized—rather than invented—the canon of Scripture.

- The Holy Ghost is essential for understanding spiritual truth.

- Bishop C. H. Mason emphasized the authority of Scripture and the need for believers to rely on both **the Word** and **the Spirit.**

Because God inspired His Word and preserved it, we can trust it fully. The Bible you hold in your hands today is God's message to you—*reliable, powerful, eternal,* and *alive.*

# REFLECTIVE QUESTIONS

1. What does it mean to you personally that the Bible is inspired by God and not written by human ideas alone?

2. How does understanding God's preservation of Scripture strengthen your confidence in the Bible?

3. Why is the Holy Ghost essential in helping believers understand the meaning of Scripture?

4. What new insight did you learn about how the early church recognized the books of the Bible?

5. How can you improve your daily relationship with the Word of God so it becomes a consistent guide for your faith and decisions?

## PRAYER

Father, I thank You for giving me Your holy and inspired Word. Thank You for preserving the Scriptures so that I can know Your truth and walk in Your will.

Holy Ghost, open my understanding, teach me as I read, and let Your Word take root in my heart.

Strengthen my faith in the reliability of the Bible and give me a greater desire to study and obey it every day.

**In Jesus' Name, Amen.**

# CHAPTER 3 - THE FIRST PRINCIPLES OF THE FAITH

Every believer must understand the basic doctrines that form the foundation of the Christian life. These are not deep theological theories, but simple, essential truths that every new believer — and every seasoned saint — should know and be able to explain.

This chapter introduces **three major sections,** each building on the one before it:

1. **The Romans Road — God's Plan of Salvation**

2. **Eternal Judgment — Why Salvation Matters**

3. **The Foundational Doctrines — How We Grow After Salvation**

Together, these three sections provide a clear picture of what it means to be saved, why eternity matters, and how a believer should grow in their walk with God.

## SECTION 1 — THE ROMANS ROAD TO SALVATION

The **"Romans Road"** is a collection of key Scriptures from the Book of Romans that explain, step by step, the message of the gospel.

It is simple, powerful, and easy to remember. For new believers, it provides clarity. For seasoned saints, it provides structure and confidence when sharing the faith.

Let us walk this road together.

## 1. Romans 3:23 — The Doctrine of Sin

*"For all have sinned, and come short of the glory of God."*

This verse teaches us one of the most important truths in the entire Bible: every human being is a sinner. No one is exempt. No one is naturally righteous. No one measures up to the holiness and perfection of God.

Sin is not just immoral behavior or mistakes; it is the condition of the heart. It is disobedience against God. It began with Adam and Eve in the garden, and it has passed down to every generation.

**Because of sin:**

- we fall short of God's glory,

- we are separated from His presence, and

- we cannot save ourselves.

Understanding this truth is the first step toward salvation.

## 2. Romans 6:23 — The Doctrine of Death and Eternal Life

*"For the wages of sin is death; but the gift of God is eternal life through Jesus Christ our Lord."*

Sin earns a payment—a wage—and that payment is death.

## This includes:

- **Physical death** (the body dies)

- **Spiritual death** (separation from God)

- **Eternal death** (everlasting judgment)

But praise be to God, the verse does not end in judgment.

The second half reveals the heart of the gospel:

*...but the gift of God is eternal life through Jesus Christ our Lord.*

Eternal life is not earned by works, effort, or good deeds.

It is a gift—freely offered to all who will receive it.

Where sin brings death, **God brings life.**

## 3. Romans 5:8 — The Doctrine of Substitutionary Atonement

*"But God commendeth His love toward us, in that, while we were yet sinners, Christ died for us."*

Here we see the greatest demonstration of love the world has ever known. While we were still sinners—*unworthy, guilty, lost,* and *broken*—**Christ died for us.**

Jesus did not die because we were perfect.

He did not die because we were righteous.

He died because we were helpless, powerless to save ourselves.

This verse teaches the doctrine of **substitution:**

- Christ died in our place.
- He bore the penalty we deserved.
- He took our sins upon Himself.
- He satisfied the justice of God.

**This is the heart of salvation:**

Jesus died the death we should have died so that we can live the life we could never earn.

## 4. Romans 10:9–10 — The Doctrine of Repentance and Faith

*"That if thou shalt confess with thy mouth the Lord Jesus, and shalt believe in thine heart that God hath raised Him from the dead, thou shalt be saved. For with the heart man believeth unto righteousness; and with the mouth confession is made unto salvation."*

This Scripture teaches us how a person receives salvation.

It is not complicated.

It is not reserved for the educated or the religious.

It is simple and available to all.

**Salvation requires two essential responses:**

**1. Belief in the heart**

— that Jesus is Lord

— that He died for our sins

— that God raised Him from the dead

**2. Confession with the mouth**

— confessing Christ openly

— acknowledging Him as Lord and Savior

Belief without confession is incomplete.

Confession without genuine belief is empty.

Together they form saving faith, the response that brings a person into right relationship with God.

## 5. Romans 10:13 — The Doctrine of "Whosoever" Salvation

*"For whosoever shall call upon the name of the Lord shall be saved."*

This verse answers one of the most important questions in the heart of any new believer:

**"Will God save me?"**

The answer is an overwhelming yes.

- Salvation is not limited by race.

- Not limited by age.

- Not limited by background.

- Not limited by education.

- Not limited by past sins.

It is for the **whosoever.**

Anyone who calls upon the Lord in faith will be saved.

This is the open invitation of God's grace to humanity.

## 6. Being Born Again (Regeneration)

When a person believes the gospel and calls upon the Lord, something supernatural happens inside them. Jesus called it being born again.

*"Except a man be born again, he cannot see the kingdom of God."* — **John 3:3**

**Regeneration means:**

- The old life passes away.

- A new life begins.

- The Holy Ghost gives spiritual birth.

- The believer becomes a child of God.

This is not joining a church or turning over a new leaf.

It is a divine transformation.

It is the beginning of the Christian walk.

## SECTION 2 — ETERNAL JUDGMENT: THE JUDGMENT OF THE BELIEVER AND THE UNBELIEVER

After understanding God's plan of salvation through the Romans Road, the next essential doctrine is **eternal judgment.**

The Bible teaches that every person will stand before God, but not all at the same judgment.

There are two distinct judgments, each with a different purpose, audience, and outcome.

**Understanding this doctrine helps believers:**

- walk in holiness

- appreciate the seriousness of salvation

- live with eternal perspective

- serve God faithfully

- share the gospel with urgency

Let us examine these two judgments with Scripture.

## I. The Judgment Seat of Christ (for Believers)

This judgment is also called the **Bema Seat,** taken from ancient athletic games where rewards were presented.

The Judgment Seat of Christ is **not a judgment of sin.**

Christ already bore our sin on the cross **(2 Corinthians 5:21).**

We are saved by grace, not by works **(Ephesians 2:8–9).**

This judgment evaluates **our works, motives,** and **faithfulness** after salvation.

**Scripture teaches:**

We must all appear before Christ.

*"We must all appear before the judgment seat of Christ; that every one may receive the things done in his body..."*

**— 2 Corinthians 5:10**

**Our works will be tested by fire.**

*"Every man's work shall be made manifest... the fire shall try every man's work of what sort it is."*

**— 1 Corinthians 3:13**

**Faithful believers will receive reward.**

*"If any man's work abide... he shall receive a reward."*

**— 1 Corinthians 3:14**

**Some will suffer loss of reward, but not salvation.**

*"He shall suffer loss: but he himself shall be saved..."*

**— 1 Corinthians 3:15**

**Christ will judge our motives.**

*"The Lord... will bring to light the hidden things of darkness, and will make manifest the counsels of the hearts."*

**— 1 Corinthians 4:5**


**For believers, the Judgment Seat of Christ is a moment of:**

- reward

- honor

- joy

- reflection

- accountability

Not condemnation.

*"There is therefore now no condemnation to them which are in Christ Jesus…"*

**— Romans 8:1**

## II. The Great White Throne Judgment (for Unbelievers)

This judgment is for those who **rejected Christ,** died in their sins, and have no covering of grace.

**Scripture teaches:**

**All unbelievers will stand before God.**

*"I saw a great white throne, and him that sat on it... and the dead, small and great, stood before God."*

**— Revelation 20:11–12**

**The books will be opened.**

*"The books were opened... and the dead were judged out of those things..."*

— **Revelation 20:12**


**Judgment is based on their deeds and rejection of Christ.**

*"He that believeth not is condemned already..."*

— **John 3:18**


**The Book of Life decides their eternal destiny.**

*"Whosoever was not found written in the book of life was cast into the lake of fire."*

— **Revelation 20:15**

**This judgment is final.**

*"It is appointed unto men once to die, but after this the judgment."*

**— Hebrews 9:27**

The Great White Throne Judgment is solemn, final, and eternal.

There is no appeal, no mercy, and no second chance.

## III. Key Differences Between the Two Judgments

The **Judgment Seat of Christ** is for believers.

It is a judgment of **works,** not salvation.

**Scripture references:**

2 Corinthians 5:10; 1 Corinthians 3:13–15;

1 Corinthians 4:5; Romans 8:1.

Believers appear before Christ to receive **rewards** for faithful service, obedience, and labor done in love.

The **Great White Throne Judgment** is for unbelievers.

It is a judgment of sin and eternal separation from God.

**Scripture references:**

Revelation 20:11–15; John 3:18; Hebrews 9:27.

Unbelievers are judged for rejecting Christ, and because their names are not written in the Book of Life, they face eternal judgment.

**In summary:**

- **Believers** → Judgment Seat of Christ → **Rewards (2 Cor. 5:10)**

- **Unbelievers** → Great White Throne → **Eternal separation (Rev. 20:15)**

- **Believers judged for works (1 Cor. 3:13)**

- **Unbelievers judged for sin and rejection of Christ (John 3:18)**

- One judgment ends in **joy,** the other in **final sorrow**

## IV. Why This Doctrine Strengthens Spiritual Growth

**1. It motivates holy living.**

Knowing we will give an account encourages purity and obedience **(2 Peter 3:11)**.

**2. It inspires faithful service.**

Nothing done for Christ is wasted **(1 Corinthians 15:58)**.

**3. It adds urgency to evangelism.**

We understand what awaits those without Christ **(Jude 23)**.

**4. It deepens gratitude for salvation.**

We are saved from wrath and judgment through the blood of Jesus **(Romans 5:9).**

**5. It keeps eternity before our eyes.**

We live for what matters most.

This doctrine is not meant to produce fear in believers— but sobriety, reverence, focus, and gratitude.

# SECTION 3 — THE FOUNDATIONAL PRACTICES OF THE CHRISTIAN LIFE

Once a believer is born again, the Bible gives several commandments and practices that help them grow in faith and obedience. These are simple yet essential doctrines that every Christian should understand.

## 7. Water Baptism

Water baptism is an outward testimony of an inward change.

**After salvation, believers are baptized to show:**

- they have died to sin,

- been buried with Christ, and

- risen to walk in newness of life.

Baptism does not save you; Jesus saves you.

But baptism is the first step of obedience and a public declaration of faith.

## 8. Holy Ghost Baptism

After water baptism, believers should seek the baptism of the Holy Ghost.

Jesus promised that His followers would receive power:

*"Ye shall receive power, after that the Holy Ghost is come upon you."* — **Acts 1:8**

### Holy Ghost baptism gives:

- strength to resist sin

- boldness to witness

- power for holy living

- spiritual gifts for service

In COGIC heritage, Holy Ghost baptism is essential for victorious Christian living.

## 9. Holy Communion (The Lord's Supper)

Jesus commanded His disciples to remember His death through the Lord's Supper:

- The bread represents His body.
- The cup represents His blood.

Believers examine themselves, confess sins, and remember Christ's sacrifice.

Communion strengthens our faith and keeps the cross at the center of our lives.

**10. Foot Washing**

In **John 13,** Jesus washed His disciples' feet and commanded:

*Ye also ought to wash one another's feet.*

— **John 13:14**

**Foot washing teaches:**

- Humility

- Servanthood

- Unity

- love between believers

COGIC historically observes this ordinance as a reminder of Christlike service.

## 11. Holiness and Christian Living

After salvation, God calls every believer to holiness:

*Be ye holy; for I am holy.* — **1 Peter 1:16**

Holiness is not perfection.

It is separation from sin and dedication to God.

Holiness is possible because:

Christ died for us, the Holy Ghost empowers us, and the Word of God guides us.

Holiness is the believer's daily lifestyle.

## CLOSING CHARGE

You have now learned the three pillars of the Christian foundation:

**how we are saved, why salvation matters eternally, and how we grow in the faith.**

Walk in this truth with confidence.

Let your salvation remain precious.

Keep eternity before your eyes.

Build your life on **repentance, faith, obedience, sanctification, fellowship,** and **the power of the Holy Ghost.**

Grow daily.

Study faithfully.

Serve humbly.

Witness boldly.

Live with a heart fully committed to Christ.

And remember: everything you do for God will be seen, rewarded, and honored when you stand before Him.

# REFLECTIVE SUMMARY

**In this chapter we have learned:**

- The **Romans Road** reveals our need for salvation and God's plan to rescue us.

- **Eternal Judgment** teaches us that every life gives an account — believers for reward, unbelievers for final judgment.

- The **Foundational Doctrines** show us how salvation works in us and how the believer grows in sanctification, faith, obedience, and fellowship.

These truths form the core of Christian maturity and provide the strong foundation every believer must build upon.

# REFLECTIVE QUESTIONS

1. What part of the Romans Road most clearly helped you understand your salvation?

2. How does the reality of eternal judgment change the way you live each day?

3. Which foundational doctrine do you feel led to grow in more deeply right now?

4. How can you practice repentance, faith, sanctification, or spiritual disciplines more intentionally?

5. What steps can you take this week to strengthen your walk and help someone else grow in the faith?

## PRAYER

Father, in the name of Jesus,

Thank You for revealing the truth of salvation, the seriousness of eternity, and the foundations of the Christian life.

Help me walk in these truths with clarity, humility, and obedience.

Strengthen my faith, deepen my repentance, purify my motives, and empower me to grow daily.

Establish my life on Your Word and help me lead others into the same truth.

Let my heart stay faithful until the day I stand before You.

**In Jesus' Name, Amen.**

# CHAPTER 4

## WHO GOD IS: UNDERSTANDING THE NATURE OF GOD

## A SIMPLE INTRODUCTION TO THE ONE TRUE GOD

There is nothing more important in the Christian life than knowing who God is. Not simply knowing facts about Him, but understanding His nature, His character, and His heart toward us.

Every doctrine in the Bible flows from this truth. Every act of obedience, every commandment, every promise, every hope of salvation begins with God Himself.

We study the Bible to grow in our knowledge of God. We pray because we believe God hears. We repent because we have sinned against God. We walk by faith because God is trustworthy. We worship because God is worthy.

Everything in the Christian life starts and ends with God.

But in the world we live in today, knowing the one true God is more important than ever.

## We Live in a World of Many "Gods" — But Only One Is True

Today, our world is filled with false gods, false spirituality, and false deities. Some worship the universe. Some consult ancestors. Some turn to crystals, tarot, astrology, or energy. Some embrace religions that deny Jesus. Others create their own version of "god" based on feelings or personal preferences.

The names may change from generation to generation, but the truth remains the same:

**Human beings have always created gods in their own image.**

But the God of the Bible does not change.

He is not shaped by culture.

He is not defined by opinion.

He is not one god among many.

**He is the ONE TRUE GOD — the Creator of heaven and earth.**

Before there was time, God was.

Before there was creation, God existed.

Before there were angels, nations, religions, or people,

**God** was already the eternal **"I AM."**

He alone has revealed Himself through His Word.

He alone has declared what He expects of us.

He alone has the authority to judge and the power to save.

There are many beliefs in the world, but only one true God.

And as believers, it is vital that we know Him — not the god of culture, not the god of imagination, not the god of superstition — but the God of Scripture.

## I. God Is One — The Foundation of Our Faith

The first truth God gave His people is this:

*"Hear, O Israel: The LORD our God is one LORD."* — **Deuteronomy 6:4**

This is the foundation of the Christian faith.

We do not worship many gods.

We do not believe in a mixture of powers.

We do not pray to saints or ancestors.

We do not bow to idols or spiritual forces.

**There is ONE GOD.**

**He is:**

- Eternal
- Sovereign
- Holy
- all-powerful
- all-knowing
- everywhere present

He alone created all things.

He alone sustains all things.

He alone rules over all things.

This truth separates the Christian faith from every other belief system in the world.

## II. God Is Three-in-One — A Simple Understanding of the Trinity

While God is One, He has revealed Himself in three Persons:

- **God the Father**

- **God the Son (Jesus Christ)**

- **God the Holy Ghost**

Not three gods.

Not three versions of God.

Not one Person acting in three different ways.

**One God in Three Persons — eternal, equal, and united.**

This is not a mystery to confuse us, but a revelation to help us understand how God works in our lives.

**God the Father** — the source of life and authority

**God the Son** — the Savior who reveals the Father

**God the Holy Ghost** — the power who dwells within us

They work together in perfect unity.

At Jesus' baptism, the Father spoke, the Son was baptized, and the Spirit descended — all three Persons active at once.

In **Matthew 28:19,** Jesus commanded His disciples to baptize in the name of the Father, Son, and Holy Ghost — one name, three Persons.

This is the God we serve.

## III. God the Father — His Heart Toward Us

Understanding God the Father helps us grow in trust and confidence.

**God is holy**

He is perfect in purity and righteousness.

There is no sin or darkness in Him.

**God is love**

His love is unconditional, unchanging, and everlasting.

**God is faithful**

He keeps every promise.

He cannot lie.

He cannot fail.

**God is just**

He judges righteously and stands against all evil.

**God is merciful**

He forgives, restores, and shows compassion.

**God is eternal**

He has no beginning and no end.

He is the same yesterday, today, and forever.

**God is all-powerful**

Nothing is too hard for Him.

**God is all-knowing**

He sees every detail of our lives.

**God is present everywhere**

There is no place where He is not.

Knowing the heart of God builds confidence in the believer.

He is not a distant deity.

He is a loving Father.

## IV. The Attributes of God — Simple Truths That Strengthen Faith

Here are a few of God's attributes explained in simple terms:

### 1. God Is Holy

Pure, perfect, separate from all sin.

### 2. God Is Love

Everything He does flows from His love.

### 3. God Is All-Powerful

Nothing can stop His will.

## 4. God Is All-Knowing

He knows every thought, every need, every fear.

## 5. God Is Everywhere Present

He is with us in every situation.

## 6. God Does Not Change

His Word, His nature, and His promises remain the same.

## 7. God Is Wise

He knows what is best for us, even when we do not.

**8. God Is Good**

His plans are for our good and His glory.

These simple truths help believers trust God more deeply and walk with greater confidence.

## V. God Reveals Himself Through His Word

We do not guess who God is.

We do not rely on feelings or opinions.

We do not accept cultural ideas of God.

We know God because He revealed Himself in Scripture.

**Through His Word we learn:**

- His nature

- His character

- His promises

- His commandments

- His expectations

- His love for humanity

The Bible is our sure foundation for understanding God.

## VI. Why Understanding God Matters for Christian Living

**Knowing who God is:**

- strengthens faith
- deepens worship
- builds trust
- encourages obedience
- gives peace
- shapes our decisions
- protects us from false doctrine
- helps us recognize His voice

A believer who knows God will not be easily shaken.

Understanding God is not just doctrine — it is daily life.

## CLOSING CHARGE

As you continue to grow in your walk with God, never lose sight of the truth you have learned in this chapter: there is only one true and living God, and He has revealed Himself to us so that we may know Him, trust Him, and serve Him.

In a world filled with false gods, false ideas, and false spirituality, stand firm in the knowledge of the God who created heaven and earth — the God who loved you before you ever knew Him.

Worship Him with reverence. Follow Him with obedience. Trust Him with your life.

Make it your daily desire to grow in the knowledge of God. The more you know Him, the more you will love Him. The more you love Him, the more you will obey Him. And the more you obey Him, the more you will walk in the peace, strength, and confidence that only He can give.

**Let your heart say with conviction:**

*"The Lord, He is God — the only true God — and Him alone will I serve."*

## REFLECTIVE SUMMARY

In this chapter, we learned that:

- We live in a world full of false gods and spiritual deceptions, but the Bible reveals one true God.

- God is One, yet He has revealed Himself as Father, Son, and Holy Ghost — one God in three Persons.

- God the Father is holy, loving, faithful, just, merciful, powerful, and unchanging.

- The attributes of God help us understand His heart and strengthen our faith.

- God reveals Himself through His Word, not through human imagination or cultural ideas.

- Knowing who God is shapes how we live, how we worship, how we pray, and how we trust Him.

Understanding God is not just a doctrine — it is the foundation of a strong and growing Christian life.

## REFLECTIVE QUESTIONS

1. What stood out most to you about the nature of the one true God?

2. How does understanding that God is holy change the way you approach Him?

3. What attribute of God (love, faithfulness, power, mercy) strengthens you in your daily walk?

4. In what ways does knowing God as Father bring comfort or clarity to your spiritual life?

5. How can you guard your heart against the false gods and false ideas present in today's world?

## PRAYER

Father, in the name of Jesus,

I thank You for revealing Yourself to me through Your Word. You alone are God — the Creator of heaven and earth, the One who rules in power and reigns in holiness. Help me to know You more deeply, trust You more fully, and walk with You more faithfully.

Keep my heart from deception and guard my mind from false ideas. Teach me Your ways. Let Your truth guide my steps and shape my life.

Strengthen me through the Holy Ghost to worship You, honor You, and obey You.

May Your presence fill my life, and may Your character be seen in everything I do.

**In Jesus' Name, Amen.**

# CHAPTER 5 — WHO JESUS IS: UNDERSTANDING THE SON OF GOD

There is no name more precious to believers than the name Jesus. Every hope we have, every promise we cling to, every blessing we enjoy, and every victory we celebrate comes through Him.

Jesus Christ is not just a figure in Christian history—He is the foundation of our faith, the Savior of the world, and the One through whom God reveals Himself fully and personally.

To grow in the faith, every believer—young or seasoned—must know who Jesus truly is. Many people have opinions about Him. Some say He was only a prophet. Others say He was only a good teacher.

Still others believe He was simply a moral example. But the Bible teaches something far greater, far deeper, and far more life-changing:

**Jesus Christ is the Son of God, the Savior, and God made flesh.**

In this chapter, we will learn who Jesus is in simple, clear terms so that your faith may be strengthened and your walk with God made firm.

## I. Jesus Is God — The Deity of Christ

The first thing every believer must know is this:

**Jesus is not just a man — He is God.**

The Bible does not leave room for confusion.

**John 1:1** declares:

*"In the beginning was the Word, and the Word was with God, and the Word was God."*

**Verse 14** adds:

*"And the Word was made flesh, and dwelt among us..."*

Jesus existed before creation.

Jesus was not created.

Jesus has always been.


He is eternal.

He is divine.

He is God.


**Here are simple truths that show His deity:**

- **Jesus received worship**, and only God is worthy of worship.

- **Jesus forgave sins,** and only God can forgive sins.

- **Jesus claimed unity with the Father:** *"I and my Father are one."*

- **Jesus demonstrated divine power,** healing the sick, calming storms, and raising the dead.

Everything Jesus did revealed who He truly is:

**God in human form, come to save us.**

## II. Jesus Is the Son of God — What This Means

When the Bible calls Jesus the Son of God, it does not mean He is inferior or secondary. It means He:

- shares the same nature as the Father,

- is eternal and divine,

- has a unique relationship with the Father,

- is equal in power, authority, and glory.

"Son of God" is a title of **majesty,** not limitation.

**It means:**

Jesus is fully God and fully man.

He came into the world as God's perfect revelation of Himself.

If you want to know what God is like, look at Jesus.

## III. The Birth of Jesus — God Made Flesh

Jesus came into the world through a miracle — the virgin birth.

The angel Gabriel told Mary that the Holy Ghost would overshadow her and she would conceive the Son of God.

**This birth fulfilled prophecy:**

- *"A virgin shall conceive..."* **(Isaiah 7:14)**

- *"Unto us a child is born..."* **(Isaiah 9:6)**

Jesus was born in a humble manger, not in a palace.

He entered the world in simplicity, poverty, and purity — yet He carried within Himself all the fullness of God.

The birth of Jesus means God came near to us, walked among us, and revealed Himself in a way humanity had never seen.

## IV. The Life and Ministry of Jesus

The life of Jesus was unlike any life ever lived.

**He:**

- taught with divine authority

- healed every sickness and disease

- cast out unclean spirits

- opened blind eyes

- cleansed lepers

- raised the dead

- fed thousands with a few loaves and fishes

- walked on water

- showed compassion to the broken and rejected

- forgave sinners

- revealed the heart of God

He lived a sinless life, perfectly fulfilling the will of the Father.

**He came to:**

- seek and save the lost,

- preach the kingdom of God,

- destroy the works of the devil,

- show us how to live,

- and prepare the way to salvation.

Everything He did demonstrated the Father's love.

## V. The Death of Jesus — The Lamb of God

The central purpose of Jesus' life was His death.

He did not come just to teach or heal — He came to die.

**John the Baptist called Him:**

*"Behold the Lamb of God, which taketh away the sin of the world."*

**On the cross:**

- Jesus took our place.

- Jesus bore our sins.

- Jesus paid our debt.

- Jesus satisfied God's justice.

- Jesus opened the way to forgiveness.

His death was not an accident.

It was the plan of God from the beginning, so that through Christ we might receive salvation.

## VI. The Resurrection — Victory Over Sin and Death

On the third day, Jesus rose from the dead — not spiritually, but bodily.

He got up with all power in His hands.

**The resurrection proves:**

- Jesus is who He claimed to be.

- He has authority over death.

- His sacrifice was accepted by the Father

- We can have eternal life through Him.

The empty tomb is the foundation of our hope.

Because He lives, we also shall live.

## VII. The Ascension and Present Ministry of Jesus

After appearing to His disciples for forty days, Jesus ascended into heaven.

But His work did not end there.

**Today, Jesus:**

- sits at the right hand of the Father,

- intercedes for believers,

- watches over His church,

- prepares a place for us,

- and will return again.

He is not distant — He is actively involved in the lives of His people.

## VIII. The Second Coming — Jesus Will Return

The Bible teaches that Jesus will come again:

- visibly,

- powerfully,

- and gloriously.

He will judge the world, gather His people, and establish His eternal kingdom.

**This gives believers hope:**

- hope in trials,
- hope in suffering,
- hope in death,
- hope for the future.

Jesus is coming again.

And we must be ready.

## IX. Why Knowing Jesus Matters

**Knowing who Jesus is:**

- strengthens our faith,

- deepens our worship,

- anchors our salvation,

- gives purpose to our lives,

- and shapes how we live every day.

Jesus is not just part of our faith — He is our faith.

Without Jesus, there is no salvation, no forgiveness, no eternal life, and no hope.

The more you know Jesus, the more you will love Him.

The more you love Him, the more you will follow Him.

And the more you follow Him, the more your life will change.

## CLOSING CHARGE

As you grow in your understanding of Jesus, remember this:

your life will only be as strong as the foundation you build on Christ.

Let your heart be settled in this truth — Jesus is Lord.

Follow Him with confidence.

Trust Him with your whole heart.

Walk with Him daily.

And let your life reflect His love, His holiness, and His grace.

# REFLECTIVE SUMMARY

In this chapter we learned that:

- Jesus is God made flesh.

- Jesus is the eternal Son of God.

- Jesus was born of a virgin.

- Jesus lived a sinless life and revealed God to humanity.

- Jesus died for our sins as the Lamb of God.

- Jesus rose from the dead in victory.

- Jesus ascended to heaven and intercedes for us.

- Jesus will return again in glory.

Understanding who Jesus is strengthens our faith and anchors our hope.

# REFLECTIVE QUESTIONS

1. What truth about Jesus stood out to you the most in this chapter?

2. How does knowing Jesus is God strengthen your faith?

3. Why is the death of Jesus essential for your salvation?

4. What does the resurrection mean to you personally?

5. How can you grow in your relationship with Jesus this week?

## **PRAYER**

Father, in the name of Jesus,

I thank You for sending Your Son into the world to save us.

Thank You for His life, His love, His sacrifice, and His victory.

Help me to know Jesus more deeply, to trust Him more fully, and to follow Him more faithfully.

Let His character be formed in me through the power of the Holy Ghost.

Guide my steps, strengthen my faith, and keep my heart focused on Him.

**In Jesus' Name, Amen.**

# CHAPTER 6— THE HOLY GHOST: OUR HELPER, TEACHER, AND POWER

When Jesus ascended into heaven, He did not leave His people alone. He did not leave us to struggle in our own strength, to live the Christian life by willpower, or to fight spiritual battles without help. Before returning to the Father, Jesus made a precious promise:

*"I will not leave you comfortless..."*

**— John 14:18**

He promised to send **another Comforter,** the Holy Ghost — the Spirit of God who would live in us, walk with us, teach us, strengthen us, and empower us for the Christian life.

To grow in the faith, every believer must understand who the Holy Ghost is and what He does. Without Him, the Christian life is powerless. With Him, we are strengthened, guided, and equipped to live a life that honors God.

Let us now learn, in simple terms, what the Bible teaches about the Holy Ghost.

## I. Who the Holy Ghost Is

Many people think of the Holy Ghost as an energy, a feeling, or an influence. But the Bible is clear:

**The Holy Ghost is God.**

He is the **third Person of the Trinity,** equal with the Father and the Son.

He is eternal.

He is divine.

He is personal.

He speaks, teaches, leads, comforts, and empowers.

The Holy Ghost is not "it."

He is **He** — a Person with mind, will, and emotion.

**He:**

- knows all things
- searches the deep things of God
- gives spiritual gifts
- directs the church
- intercedes for believers
- can be grieved
- can be resisted

These truths help us understand that the Holy Ghost is fully God and worthy of the same honor, reverence, and obedience we give to the Father and the Son.

## II. The Holy Ghost in the Life of Jesus

Before we look at His work in our lives, it helps to see His work in the life of Jesus.

- The Holy Ghost **overshadowed Mary,** and Jesus was conceived.

- The Holy Ghost **descended on Jesus** at His baptism.

- Jesus was **led by the Spirit** into the wilderness.

- Jesus returned **in the power of the Spirit** to begin His ministry.

- Jesus cast out devils **by the Spirit of God.**

- Jesus was **raised from the dead** by the Spirit.

If Jesus — the sinless Son of God — walked in the power of the Holy Ghost, how much more do we need Him?

## III. The Work of the Holy Ghost in Salvation

The Holy Ghost is active before we ever come to Christ.

**He convicts us of sin.**

He opens our eyes to see our need for salvation.

**He draws us to Christ.**

No one can come unless the Spirit works on the heart.

**He regenerates us.**

This is the new birth — being made spiritually alive.

**He seals us.**

He marks us as God's own, securing our salvation.


These are foundational truths that every believer should know.

## IV. The Indwelling of the Holy Ghost

When a person accepts Christ, the Holy Ghost comes to live inside them.

This is called the **indwelling** of the Spirit.

**Because He lives in us:**

- He comforts us in trouble.

- He gives us strength to endure.

- He helps us pray when we don't know what to say.

- He illuminates the Scriptures.

- He reminds us of what Jesus taught.

- He guides us into truth.

- He transforms our character.

- He enables us to resist sin.


A believer who walks without the Holy Ghost walks in weakness.


A believer who walks with the Holy Ghost walks in power.

## V. The Baptism of the Holy Ghost (COGIC Teaching)

While every believer receives the Spirit at conversion, the Bible also teaches a separate, distinct experience called the **Baptism of the Holy Ghost.**

**In the Church Of God In Christ, we believe:**

- The Baptism of the Holy Ghost is for all believers.

- It is an experience that comes after salvation.

- It is accompanied by speaking in tongues as the initial physical evidence.

- It gives power for Christian living and bold witnessing.

- It was promised by Jesus and poured out on Pentecost.

**Jesus told His disciples:**

*"Ye shall receive power, after that the Holy Ghost is come upon you…"*

**— Acts 1:8**

This baptism does not make a believer "better" than others — it makes a believer better equipped.

It fills us with boldness, spiritual strength, and deeper devotion to God.

## VI. The Fruit of the Spirit — The Character of Christ in Us

When the Holy Ghost lives within us, He begins producing spiritual "fruit" in our lives — qualities that reflect the character of Christ.

**From Galatians 5:22–23:**

**1. Love** — choosing to care and act with compassion.

**2. Joy** — deep gladness that does not depend on circumstances.

**3. Peace** — calm assurance in God's control.

**4. Longsuffering** — patience in difficult situations.

**5. Gentleness** — softness and kindness in dealing with others.

**6. Goodness** — doing what is right and honorable.

**7. Faith** — reliability, loyalty, and trustworthiness.

**8. Meekness** — strength under control.

**9. Temperance** — self-control in thoughts and actions.

These qualities are not produced by our own strength.

They are the result of the Holy Ghost working in us.

## VII. The Gifts of the Spirit — Empowerment for Ministry

The Holy Ghost also gives **spiritual gifts** to build up the church.

**Some of these gifts include:**

- Wisdom
- Knowledge
- Faith
- Healing
- Miracles
- Prophecy

- Discernment

- Tongues

- interpretation of tongues

**These gifts:**

- strengthen the church,

- help the saints grow,

- and bring glory to God.

Gifts are not for personal praise — they are for **service.**

## VIII. Walking in the Spirit — Daily Christian Living

**Walking in the Spirit means:**

- obeying God's voice

- surrendering our desires

- resisting temptation

- seeking God through prayer

- reading the Word faithfully

- worshipping wholeheartedly

- staying in fellowship with the saints

When we walk in the Spirit, the flesh loses its power.

When we ignore the Spirit, the flesh grows stronger.

**The Holy Ghost empowers us to:**

- live holy,

- walk uprightly,

- and reflect Christ in our daily conduct.

## CLOSING CHARGE

Believer, you cannot grow in the faith without the Holy Ghost.

You cannot overcome temptation, live holy, or walk in victory apart from His power.

Allow the Holy Ghost to fill your life.

Yield to His leading.

Obey His voice.

Let Him strengthen your heart, direct your path, and transform your character.

Jesus promised we would receive power.

That power is the Holy Ghost.


Seek Him.

Welcome Him.

Surrender to Him.

And let Him lead you into a deeper, stronger, more confident walk with God.

## REFLECTIVE SUMMARY

**In this chapter we learned that:**

- The Holy Ghost is God, the third Person of the Trinity.

- He was present in the life and ministry of Jesus.

- He convicts, draws, regenerates, and seals us.

- He dwells within every believer.

- The Baptism of the Holy Ghost is a separate, powerful experience for believers.

- He produces spiritual fruit in our lives.

- He gives gifts for ministry.

- He empowers us to walk in holiness and obedience.

The Holy Ghost is our Helper, Teacher, Strengthener, and Guide.

## REFLECTIVE QUESTIONS

1. What truth about the Holy Ghost helped you the most in this chapter?

2. How does the indwelling of the Holy Ghost give you confidence in your Christian walk?

3. Why is the Baptism of the Holy Ghost important for believers today?

4. Which fruit of the Spirit do you desire to grow in more deeply?

5. What steps can you take to walk more consistently in the Spirit?

## **PRAYER**

Father, in the name of Jesus,

I thank You for the gift of the Holy Ghost.

Thank You for sending Your Spirit to live in me, teach me, strengthen me, and guide me.

Fill me with Your power.

Lead me into all truth.

Produce Your fruit in my life and help me walk in holiness.

Baptize me anew with the Holy Ghost and fire, and empower me to be a bold witness for Christ.

**In Jesus' Name, Amen.**

# CHAPTER 7 — HOLY LIVING: GROWING IN OBEDIENCE

When a person gives their life to Jesus Christ, everything changes. Salvation is not only about escaping judgment or going to heaven one day. It is the beginning of a new life—a life shaped by *obedience, guided by the Holy Ghost*, and *marked by a growing desire to please God*.

Holy living is not something we achieve in our own strength. It is something God produces in us as we surrender to Him day by day. It is the outward expression of an inward transformation. When Christ saves us, He does not leave us the way He found us. He begins a work within us that continues for the rest of our lives.

This chapter will explain, in simple terms, what holy living means, why it matters, and how every believer—new or seasoned—can grow in obedience to God.

## I. What Holy Living Means in Simple Terms

Many people misunderstand holiness. Some think it means perfection, which is impossible. Others think it means strict rules or outward appearance, which leads to legalism. But holy living, according to the Bible, is much simpler and much deeper.

**Holy living means living a life that honors God.**

**It is:**

- obeying God's Word,

- resisting sin,

- opening your heart to the Holy Ghost,

- allowing God to shape your character,

- and separating yourself from things that pull you away from Him.

Holiness is not about being better than others. It is about becoming more like Jesus.

## II. Why Holiness Is Essential for Every Believer

God calls His people to live holy lives because:

### 1. God is holy.

*"Be ye holy; for I am holy."* — **1 Peter 1:16**

Holiness reflects God's nature.

We cannot walk with a holy God and cling to unholy living.

### 2. Jesus died to free us from sin.

Salvation delivers us from the penalty of sin,

but holiness delivers us from the power of sin.

**3. Holiness protects us from destruction.**

Sin leads to bondage,

but holiness leads to freedom.


**4. Holiness strengthens our witness.**

People may never read a Bible,

but they will read your life.


**5. Holiness pleases God.**

A holy life is an offering of gratitude to the One who saved us.

## III. Holiness Is Not Instant — It Is a Lifelong Walk

When we are saved, we belong to God instantly.

But becoming like Christ is a lifelong journey.

**There are two sides to holiness:**

**1. Instant holiness (our position in Christ).**

God sees us as righteous because of Jesus.

**2. Progressive holiness (our daily growth).**

The Holy Ghost helps us overcome sin, develop new habits, and grow into spiritual maturity.

This keeps believers encouraged.

We are growing, learning, and becoming stronger—not overnight, but over time.

## IV. The Role of the Holy Ghost in Holy Living

The Holy Ghost is the power behind holy living.

We cannot live holy in our own strength.

**He enables us to:**

- resist temptation,
- love our enemies,
- forgive those who hurt us,
- walk in obedience,
- desire the things of God,

- and turn away from the things that once controlled us.

The Holy Ghost does not only convict us of sin—

He **empowers** us to overcome it.

This makes the Christian life joyful instead of burdensome.

## V. The Word of God and Holy Living

You cannot live holy without the Word of God.

**The Word:**

- cleanses the heart,

- renews the mind,

- strengthens the spirit,

- exposes sin,

- reveals truth,

- teaches righteousness,

- and guides our decisions.

**Jesus said:**

*"Sanctify them through thy truth: thy word is truth."*

**— John 17:17**

Holiness grows in the soil of Scripture.

## VI. The Importance of Repentance in Holy Living

Repentance is not only for new believers.

It is part of our daily walk with God.

**Repentance:**

- keeps the heart soft and humble,

- restores fellowship with God,

- cleanses the conscience,

- protects us from spiritual blindness,

- and strengthens our desire to walk uprightly.

A believer who refuses to repent will stop growing.

A believer who practices repentance will flourish.

## VII. Separating From the Old Life

Holy living requires a break from certain patterns of the past.

**This may involve:**

- new friendships,

- healthier environments,

- different habits,

- better influences,

- and intentional choices.

Separation does not mean isolation.

It means guarding your spiritual health.

Anything that weakens your walk with God must be given up.

Anything that draws you closer to God must be embraced.

## VIII. Walking in Spiritual Discipline

Holiness is strengthened through spiritual disciplines such as:

### Prayer

It keeps the heart tender and tuned to God's voice.

### Reading Scripture

It renews the mind and strengthens obedience.

### Fasting

It helps the believer crucify the flesh and hear God clearly.

**Attending Church**

We grow when we stay connected to the body of Christ.

**Fellowship**

Other believers strengthen our faith and keep us accountable.

**Serving**

Serving develops humility, compassion, and spiritual maturity.

Holy living grows through consistent spiritual habits.

## IX. The Rewards of Holy Living

Holy living brings blessings into the life of every believer.

### 1. Peace

God guards the mind and heart.

### 2. Joy

Holiness produces joy that circumstances cannot take away.

### 3. Spiritual authority

A holy life carries weight in the spiritual realm.

### 4. Growth

Holiness strengthens spiritual maturity.

### 5. Answered prayer

Obedience opens the door for God to move.

### 6. Protection

Holiness keeps believers from destructive paths.

### 7. Clarity

A holy life makes it easier to hear God's voice.

Holiness is not a burden.

It is a blessing.

## CLOSING CHARGE

Believer, God has called you to a life of holiness—not by force, but by love. Holiness is not a punishment; it is a privilege. It is the evidence that Jesus lives in you.

Walk with God daily. Obey His Word. Yield to the Holy Ghost. Turn away from anything that weakens your spiritual life.

Let your heart declare, *"Lord, make me more like You,"* and He will

# REFLECTIVE SUMMARY

**In this chapter, we learned:**

- Holiness is living a life that honors God.

- God calls every believer to live holy.

- Holiness is both instant (at salvation) and progressive (through growth).

- The Holy Ghost empowers us to live holy.

- The Word cleanses and guides us.

- Repentance is essential for spiritual health.

- Holiness requires separating from sin and walking in discipline.

- Holy living brings peace, joy, and spiritual strength.

Holiness is not about perfection—it is about direction.

It is choosing Jesus daily.

# REFLECTIVE QUESTIONS

1. What area of your life is the Holy Ghost calling you to surrender or strengthen?

2. How does the Word of God help you grow in holiness?

3. Why is repentance necessary for spiritual growth?

4. What spiritual discipline do you need to practice more consistently?

5. How has God already begun transforming your life since salvation?

## PRAYER

Father, in the name of Jesus,

Thank You for calling me to a life of holiness.

Help me to walk in obedience, honor Your Word, and surrender my heart fully to You.

Strengthen me through the Holy Ghost to resist sin, grow in maturity, and live a life that reflects Your character.

Cleanse me daily, guide me faithfully, and shape me into the image of Christ.

**In Jesus' Name, Amen.**

# CHAPTER 8 — WORSHIP & PRAYER: DRAWING NEAR TO GOD

Every believer desire to grow in their walk with God, but growth does not begin with activity—it begins with relationship. And relationship with God is strengthened through **two simple but powerful practices:**

**Worship**

**Prayer**

These are not religious rituals.

They are the heartbeat of the Christian life.

Worship is how we recognize who God is.

Prayer is how we communicate with Him.

A believer who learns to worship and pray will grow strong.

A believer who neglects worship and prayer will remain weak, confused, and unfocused.

This chapter will teach, in simple terms, how to develop a strong life of worship and prayer.

## I. What Worship Really Is

Many think worship is the slow song during church service.

Some think worship is just lifting hands.

Others think worship is emotional expression.

But worship is far deeper.

**At its core:**

Worship is the act of giving God His rightful place in your heart.

**It means:**

- honoring God above everything else

- valuing His presence

- responding to His goodness

- submitting to His will

- loving Him with all your heart

Worship touches the entire life—

not only what you sing,

but how you live.

## II. Why Worship Matters for Every Believer

Worship is essential because:

**1. God created us for worship.**

Everything in creation praises Him.

**2. Worship brings us into God's presence.**

*"In Thy presence is fullness of joy."*

**3. Worship changes spiritual atmosphere.**

Where God is honored, darkness flees.

**4. Worship softens the heart.**

A worshiping heart is a listening heart.

**5. Worship aligns us with God's will.**

It places God above our desires and struggles.

Worship strengthens faith, calms fear, lifts burdens, and opens the heart to receive from God.

## III. The Heart of Worship: It Begins With Love

**True worship is not about:**

- talent

- volume

- emotion

- performance

**Worship flows from:**

- gratitude

- love

- surrender

- trust

- obedience

**Jesus said:**

*"The true worshipers shall worship the Father in spirit and in truth."*

**— John 4:23**

***"Spirit"*** — from the heart, not just the lips.

***"Truth"*** — according to God's Word, not our opinion.

Worship begins with knowing who God is and responding to His greatness.

## IV. What Prayer Is: Talking and Listening to God

Prayer is simply **communication with God.**

**It is:**

- talking to God
- listening for His guidance
- expressing your heart
- seeking His will
- thanking Him for His goodness
- asking for His help

Prayer is not complicated.

It does not require flowery language.

It is not measured by length or volume.

**Prayer is a child speaking with their Father.**

God desires conversation with you.

## V. Why Prayer Is Essential

Prayer is the believer's lifeline.

**It is how we:**

- receive strength
- gain direction
- overcome temptation
- grow spiritually
- find peace
- stay connected to God
- receive answers

- walk in power

Jesus Himself prayed regularly.

If the Son of God needed prayer, how much more do we?

## VI. How to Pray: A Simple Model for New Believers

Here is an easy way to pray daily:

### 1. Start with Praise (Worship)

*"Lord, I honor You. I thank You for who You are."*

### 2. Surrender Your Will

*"Have Your way in my life today."*

### 3. Confess Your Sins

*"Forgive me for anything that displeased You."*

## 4. Present Your Needs

*"Lord, here is what I am facing..."*

## 5. Pray for Others

*"Bless my family, church, and those who need You."*

## 6. Give Thanks

*"Thank You for hearing and answering."*

## 7. Listen

*Sit quietly. Allow the Holy Ghost to speak to your heart.*

This simple pattern develops a powerful prayer life.

## VII. The Holy Ghost Helps Us Pray

Sometimes we don't know what to say.

**The Holy Ghost:**

- gives us the words

- stirs our hearts

- strengthens our faith

- leads us in what to pray

- prays through us

**Romans 8:26** teaches that the Spirit helps our weakness and intercedes for us.

Prayer becomes powerful when the Holy Ghost leads.

## VIII. Making Worship and Prayer Part of Daily Life

New believers should not wait for Sunday to worship.

**Worship and prayer should happen:**

- at home
- in the car
- during work breaks
- early in the morning
- before bed

**Here are simple habits:**

**Set a daily prayer time.**

Even 5–10 minutes is powerful.

**Begin the day with worship music or Scripture.**

It sets your spirit in the right direction.

**Pray before decisions.**

Large and small.

**End the day with gratitude.**

A thankful heart invites God's presence.

These simple practices build strong spiritual roots.

## IX. Worship & Prayer in the Life of a Growing Believer

**As you grow spiritually:**

- worship becomes more personal

- prayer becomes more natural

- the Holy Ghost's voice becomes clearer

- Scripture becomes more alive

- your relationship with God deepens

A praying believer is a powerful believer.

A worshiping believer is a peaceful believer.

A believer who does both is unstoppable.

## CLOSING CHARGE

Make worship and prayer your first work every day.

Not out of duty, but out of love.

Let your heart rise to God in praise.

Let your voice call out to Him in prayer.

Let your ears open to His gentle whisper.

Worship will change your heart.

Prayer will change your life.

Together, they will draw you closer to God than you have ever been.

# REFLECTIVE SUMMARY

**In this chapter, we learned:**

- Worship is honoring God with your whole heart.

- Prayer is communication with God—talking and listening.

- Worship brings us into God's presence.

- Prayer strengthens us for daily life.

- The Holy Ghost helps us pray.

- Praying in the Spirit builds up the believer.

- Worship and prayer must become daily habits.

A believer who worships and prays will grow strong in faith.

# REFLECTIVE QUESTIONS

1. What does worship mean to you personally after reading this chapter?

2. How can you make prayer a consistent part of your daily life?

3. What areas of your life need God's touch through prayer?

4. How has the Holy Ghost helped you pray when you felt weak or unsure?

5. What is one way you can deepen your worship this week?

## PRAYER

Father, in the name of Jesus,

Teach me to worship You with all my heart.

Draw me into Your presence daily.

Help me to pray with sincerity, faith, and expectation.

Fill me with the Holy Ghost and guide my thoughts as I seek Your face.

Let my worship be pure and my prayer life be strong.

May I walk closely with You every day.

**In Jesus' Name, Amen.**

# CHAPTER 9 — THE CHURCH: FELLOWSHIP, GATHERING, AND THE FAMILY OF GOD

When a person gives their life to Christ, they are not only saved from sin — they are brought into a family. They become part of something larger than themselves: the Body of Christ, the Household of Faith, the Church.

In today's world, many believers try to serve God alone. Some avoid church because of past experiences. Others think they can grow without gathering with the saints. But God never designed the Christian life to be lived in isolation.

A believer without a church home is a believer without support, covering, accountability, or spiritual nourishment.

In this chapter we will learn why the Church is essential to spiritual growth and how fellowship strengthens, guides, and protects the believer.

## I. What the Church Is — A Simple Explanation

**The Church is not:**

- a building
- a denomination
- a Sunday routine
- or a social club

**The Church is:**

**1. God's Family**

Everyone who believes in Jesus becomes part of God's household.

**2. The Body of Christ**

Every believer is a member with a purpose and function.

**3. A Spiritual Community**

A gathering of people redeemed by God, worshiping together, growing together, serving together.

## 4. A Place of Teaching and Truth

Where the Word of God is taught and understood.

## 5. A House of Prayer, Worship, and Fellowship

The Church is God's idea, not man's.

It is where His people gather to meet with Him and with one another.

## II. Why Every Believer Needs the Church

New believers — and even older saints — must understand this clearly:

### 1. God Commands Us to Gather

*"Not forsaking the assembling of ourselves together..."*
**— Hebrews 10:25**

Gathering is not optional — it is obedience.

## 2. The Church Strengthens Our Faith

Worship lifts burdens.

Teaching builds understanding.

Fellowship encourages the heart.

## 3. The Church Protects Us From Spiritual Danger

**Isolation makes believers vulnerable:**

- to discouragement

- to temptation

- to false doctrine

- to spiritual weakness

A disconnected believer becomes an easy target for the enemy.

**4. The Church Helps Us Grow**

**We grow in:**

- knowledge (teaching)
- character (accountability)
- maturity (ministry)
- love (relationships)

## 5. The Church Is a Place of Healing and Support

**In the house of God, people:**

- pray for one another

- comfort one another

- restore one another

- encourage one another

No believer is meant to walk alone.

## III. The Role of Pastors, Teachers, and Spiritual Leaders

God gave leaders to the Church for a purpose.

### Pastors

Shepherd the flock, feed the Word, guide, correct, and protect.

### Teachers

Explain the Scriptures so believers understand truth.

### Evangelists

Proclaim the gospel and stir the church to soul-winning.

### Prophets

Speak God's direction and warn of danger.

**The Fivefold Ministry**

**(From Ephesians 4:11–12)**

exists to build up the church so believers grow into spiritual maturity.

A believer grows best under sound leadership — leadership that teaches truth and lives it.

## IV. Why Fellowship Is Essential

Fellowship means sharing life together.

**In the early church, believers:**

- prayed together

- ate together

- worshiped together

- studied the Word together

- supported one another

- served together

Fellowship keeps the believer rooted, encouraged, inspired, and accountable.

Without fellowship, faith weakens.

With fellowship, faith grows strong.

## V. The Dangers of Trying to Serve God Alone

A believer who tries to live the Christian life alone will eventually struggle **with:**

- loneliness

- lack of accountability

- confusion about doctrine

- spiritual dryness

- discouragement

- temptation

- emotional isolation

**Even the strongest believer needs:**

- teaching
- prayer support
- correction
- encouragement
- community

Christianity is a **we** faith, not a me faith.

## VI. The Blessings of Church Involvement

Here are the blessings God gives through a **healthy church:**

- Growth through the Word
- Strength through fellowship
- Power through corporate worship
- Healing through prayer
- Encouragement through relationships
- Direction through spiritual leadership
- Protection from false teaching
- Opportunities for service
- Community during crisis

There are blessings you cannot receive unless you are connected to a local church.

## VII. What to Look for in a Church

A believer should **look for:**

### 1. Sound biblical teaching

The Word must be preached clearly and truthfully.

### 2. A Christ-centered focus

The church must exalt Jesus.

### 3. The presence and freedom of the Holy Ghost

A church must be alive, not dead.

**4. Love among the people**

A church without love is spiritually sick.

**5. Accountability and structure**

A church should help you grow.

**6. Opportunities to serve**

Every believer should be able to use their gifts.

A good church helps believers become strong disciples.

## VIII. Staying Connected and Committed

Many believers attend church but do not stay consistent.

Growth requires commitment.

**Here are simple steps for staying connected:**

- Attend regularly
- Join a ministry or small group
- Be faithful in prayer and giving
- Build relationships with other believers
- Support your pastor
- Serve where needed
- Receive correction humbly

A planted believer becomes a fruitful believer.

## IX. The Church as a Place of Mission

The Church is not only a place to grow — it is a place to be sent out.

- We learn inside the church.

- We witness outside the church.

- We worship together.

- We serve the world.

The Church is God's instrument for reaching the lost.

## CLOSING CHARGE

Believer, God has placed you in His family for a reason.

You cannot reach your full spiritual potential without the Church.

Fellowship will strengthen you.

Teaching will guide you.

Worship will lift you.

Community will support you.

Service will mature you.

Choose to stay planted.

Choose to stay connected.

Choose to grow with God's people.

A growing believer is a gathering believer.

# REFLECTIVE SUMMARY

**In this chapter we learned that:**

- The Church is God's family and Christ's body.

- Every believer needs fellowship and gathering.

- Pastors and leaders help us grow spiritually.

- Isolation is dangerous and weakens faith.

- The Church provides teaching, support, healing, and accountability.

- Staying committed to a church strengthens maturity.

The Church is not optional — **it is essential.**

# REFLECTIVE QUESTIONS

1. Why is the Church important for your spiritual growth?

2. How has fellowship encouraged or strengthened you in the past?

3. What qualities should you look for in a church home?

4. What steps can you take to stay more connected and committed to your church?

5. How can you use your gifts to strengthen your local church community?

## PRAYER

Father, in the name of Jesus,

Thank You for placing me in the Body of Christ.

Thank You for the Church, for fellowship, and for spiritual family.

Help me to stay committed, rooted, and connected.

Guide me to a church home where I can grow, serve, and be strengthened.

Teach me to love Your people and walk in unity.

Help me honor You through my commitment to the household of faith.

**In Jesus' Name, Amen.**

# CHAPTER 10 — SPIRITUAL GROWTH & MATURITY: GROWING UP IN CHRIST

Every believer begins their journey as a newborn in the faith.

No one is born spiritually mature — maturity is developed over time as we walk with God, obey His Word, and submit to the leading of the Holy Ghost.

Just as a child grows physically, a Christian must grow spiritually.

**Growth is not automatic. It requires:**

- desire,

- discipline,

- patience,

- consistency,

- and daily dependence on God.

**Spiritual maturity is not measured by:**

- how long you have been saved,

- how loud you shout,

- or how often you attend church.

It is measured by **Christlike character,** consistent obedience, and a heart that seeks God above all else.

This chapter will gently guide the believer in understanding what spiritual growth is, why it matters, and how to grow strong in the Lord.

# I. What Spiritual Growth Really Means

Spiritual growth is the process of becoming more like Jesus.

**It is the steady development of:**

- faith,

- character,

- understanding,

- and obedience.

**A mature believer:**

- responds to trials with faith, not fear,

- pursues holiness, not compromise,

- loves others, not grudges,

- seeks God's will, not their own,

- and stands firm in truth, not tossed by every wind of doctrine.

Growth is a journey, not a race.

And God desires every believer to grow.

## II. Why Spiritual Growth Is Necessary

Many believers remain spiritually weak because they were never taught that growth is part of the Christian life.

**Spiritual growth is essential because:**

**1. It strengthens our faith.**

A mature believer is not easily shaken.

**2. It stabilizes our emotions.**

Growth produces patience, wisdom, and self-control.

### 3. It helps us overcome sin.

The Holy Ghost strengthens us to resist temptation.

### 4. It prepares us for service.

God develops us before He uses us.

### 5. It protects us from false teaching.

A mature believer can discern truth from error.

God never intended us to remain spiritual infants.

He calls us to grow up into Christ.

## III. The Stages of Spiritual Growth

The Bible presents growth in **three easy-to-understand stages:**

### 1. Infants (New Believers)

Hungry for milk — basic teachings about salvation, prayer, and the Bible.

### 2. Young Men/Women (Growing Believers)

Learning to overcome the enemy, developing habits of obedience, and gaining strength through the Word.

### 3. Fathers/Mothers (Mature Believers)

Those who know God deeply, walk in wisdom, and help others grow.

Everyone is somewhere on this journey.

The goal is not perfection — but progress.

## IV. How God Helps Us Grow

Spiritual growth is not something we do alone.

God Himself works in us.

### 1. The Holy Ghost develops our character.

He convicts, corrects, comforts, teaches, and strengthens.

### 2. The Word of God feeds us.

Scripture renews our minds, builds faith, and reveals truth.

### 3. Prayer deepens our relationship with God.

Daily fellowship helps us grow closer to Him.

**4. Trials and challenges mature us.**

God uses difficulties to develop patience, endurance, and trust.

**5. Fellowship with believers encourages growth.**

We grow better when we walk with others in the faith.

Growth is a partnership —

God works in us, and we respond in obedience.

## V. Signs of Spiritual Maturity

**A believer is growing when they begin to:**

- respond with love instead of anger

- forgive quickly

- obey without hesitation

- stay faithful to church

- study the Word consistently

- pray regularly

- resist temptation with increasing strength

- show self-control

- walk in humility

- seek God's will above their own

Maturity is seen not only in what you know — but in how you live.

## VI. What Hinders Spiritual Growth

Some believers struggle for years because they do not recognize the things that slow or stop their growth.

**Common hindrances include:**

### 1. Neglecting the Word

No believer can grow apart from Scripture.

### 2. Prayerlessness

A prayerless life is a powerless life.

### 3. Inconsistent church attendance

Growth requires teaching, fellowship, and accountability.

### 4. Unconfessed sin

Sin weakens the believer's walk and steals spiritual strength.

### 5. Wrong relationships

Ungodly influences pull believers backward.

### 6. Laziness or lack of discipline

Growth requires intentional effort.

## 7. Emotional immaturity

Refusing correction or holding grudges keeps believers stuck.

Recognizing these hindrances is the first step to overcoming them.

## VII. How to Grow Spiritually (A Simple Path for Every Believer)

Here is a clear, practical plan for **growing in the faith:**

**1. Make time for God daily.**

Even 10 minutes can establish consistency.

**2. Read and listen to the Scripture regularly.**

Milk for beginners — meat as you grow.

**3. Pray with sincerity and expectation.**

Talk to God about your struggles and desires.

**4. Stay connected to your church.**

Teaching + fellowship = strength.

**5. Obey quickly when God speaks.**

Delayed obedience is disobedience.

**6. Confess and forsake sin immediately.**

Keeping your heart clean helps you grow.

**7. Surround yourself with believers who encourage growth.**

You rise to the level of those you walk with.

**8. Use your spiritual gifts when opportunities come.**

Serving others strengthens your faith.

Growth happens gradually —

but it happens surely when these habits are practiced.

## VIII. Growing Through Trials

Trials are not signs of God's abandonment — they are invitations to spiritual maturity.

**God uses trials to:**

- strengthen faith

- teach endurance

- deepen trust

- develop character

- reveal areas needing growth

- make us more like Jesus

Spiritual maturity is not developed on the mountaintop — it is refined in the valley.

**A mature believer learns to say:**

*"Lord, I don't understand it, but I trust You."*

That is growth.

## IX. Helping Believers Grow: A Simple Framework for Spiritual Evaluation

Just as soldiers in the Army receive evaluations to identify strengths and weaknesses so they can grow, many believers need the same kind of guidance in their spiritual walk.

Not criticism — guidance.

Spiritual evaluation is not about judging someone's salvation.

It is about helping believers see where they are spiritually and where God desires them to grow next.

Every believer benefits from honest reflection.

Every church benefits when its members grow on purpose.

This simple framework can help any believer — and any pastor or teacher — reflect on spiritual progress.

## 1. Faithfulness

Consistency in worship, prayer, study, and church attendance.

## 2. Hunger for the Word

A desire to understand and apply Scripture.

### 3. Prayer Life

Regular, sincere communication with God.

### 4. Character and Conduct

Christlike attitudes and behaviors.

### 5. Teachability

Humility in receiving instruction and correction.

### 6. Relationships

Forgiveness, unity, kindness, and peace with others.

## 7. Service

A willingness to help, volunteer, and bless the church.

## 8. Emotional Stability

Handling trials with calmness and faith.

## 9. Consistency

Steadiness in your walk with God.

## 10. Responsibility

Reliability, follow-through, and accountability.

This evaluation is a tool — not a test.

It helps believers see where they are growing and where God may be calling them deeper.

## CLOSING CHARGE

Grow on purpose.

Do not settle for spiritual infancy.

Let God develop your heart, strengthen your faith, and mature your character.

Choose daily habits that honor God.

Walk in obedience, depend on the Holy Ghost, and allow the Word to shape your life.


A growing believer becomes a strong believer — and a strong believer becomes a vessel God can use.

# REFLECTIVE SUMMARY

**In this chapter we learned:**

- Spiritual growth is becoming more like Christ.

- Growth is essential for stability, maturity, and strength.

- God uses His Word, prayer, fellowship, and trials to develop us.

- Spiritual maturity is seen in character, obedience, and love.

- Believers grow intentionally through daily spiritual habits.

- A simple evaluation can reveal where we are growing and where we need to improve.

Spiritual maturity is not a destination — it is a lifelong journey with God.

## REFLECTIVE QUESTIONS

1. In what areas do you feel God is calling you to grow right now?

2. What habits can you strengthen to help your spiritual development?

3. What hindrances have slowed your growth in the past?

4. How has God used trials to mature you spiritually?

5. What did the spiritual evaluation reveal about your strengths and weaknesses?

# PRAYER

Father, in the name of Jesus,

Help me to grow in grace and in the knowledge of Your Word.

Strengthen my faith, deepen my love, and shape my character.

Remove anything that hinders my growth.

Teach me to walk in obedience and depend on the Holy Ghost.

Make me more like Christ in my thoughts, words, and actions.

**In Jesus' Name, Amen.**

# CHAPTER 11 — WITNESSING & WINNING SOULS: SHARING THE FAITH WITH CONFIDENCE

Every believer is called to share the good news of Jesus Christ.

Not only pastors, not only evangelists, not only teachers — every believer.

Witnessing is not about having a title. It is not about standing on a street corner. It is not about arguing people into salvation.

Witnessing is simply telling someone what Jesus has done for you — and what He can do for them.

When a believer understands salvation, grows spiritually, and walks with God daily, the next natural step is to share that faith with others.

A silent Christian in a suffering world is a contradiction.

God has given every believer a voice and a story, and He intends for us to use them for His glory.

## I. Why Witnessing Matters

Many believers hesitate to share their faith because they feel unprepared, nervous, or unsure of what to say.

But witnessing is not difficult. The enemy simply wants to silence us.

**Here is why witnessing is essential:**

1. Jesus Commanded It

*"Go ye into all the world and preach the gospel..."*

**— Mark 16:15**

Witnessing is not optional — **it is obedience.**

## 2. Souls Are at Stake

People are lost without Christ — and God uses believers to reach them.

## 3. Someone Once Witnessed to You

We are saved today because someone cared enough to tell us about Jesus.

## 4. The Gospel Is the Power of God

When we share the message, the Holy Ghost touches the heart.

## 5. Witnessing Strengthens Your Own Faith

Every time you speak of Jesus, your confidence grows.

## II. What the Gospel Is — A Simple Explanation for All Believers

Before we witness, we must know what we are sharing.

**The gospel is:**

### 1. God's Love for Humanity

He created us for relationship.

### 2. Man's Problem: Sin

All have sinned **(Romans 3:23).**

Sin separates us from God.

### 3. God's Solution: Jesus Christ

Jesus died in our place **(Romans 5:8)**,

rose again,

and offers forgiveness.

### 4. Our Response

**We must:**

- Repent
- Believe
- confess Christ
- and receive salvation

This is the gospel in its simplest form.

A believer does not need a theology degree to share this.

## III. How to Share Your Faith Naturally

Witnessing does not require pressure, fear, or force. It should flow naturally from a life transformed by Christ.

**Here are simple, practical ways to witness:**

### 1. Share Your Testimony

Tell what God has done for you — briefly and sincerely.

### 2. Share Scripture

A simple verse can open the heart.

### 3. Share Hope

Many people are hurting. Encouragement opens doors.

### 4. Share Jesus in Everyday Moments

At work, school, the store, or at home — opportunities appear when our hearts are ready.

### 5. Invite Someone to Church

Your church is part of your witness.

The simplest witness can change someone's eternity.

## IV. The Power of the Holy Ghost in Witnessing

We do not witness in our own strength.

God empowers us.

### 1. The Holy Ghost Gives Boldness

Timid believers become courageous witnesses.

### 2. The Holy Ghost Gives the Words

He brings Scripture to your mind at the right moment.

### 3. The Holy Ghost Opens Hearts

You speak — but He convicts, draws, and saves.

## 4. The Holy Ghost Confirms the Message

Sometimes with peace, tears, conviction, or understanding.

A believer filled with the Holy Ghost is a powerful witness.

## V. Overcoming Fear and Hesitation

Almost all believers fear witnessing at first.

But the fear fades **when we remember:**

**1. We are not responsible for saving people — only sharing the message.**

God does the saving.

**2. Most people are more open than we think.**

Many are searching for hope.

**3. You can start small.**

A smile, a prayer, an invitation — all are seeds.

**4. God will guide you to the right people.**

He places people in our path intentionally.

Fear disappears as confidence grows.

## VI. Practical Ways to Witness Every Day

To help new believers, here are **simple methods:**

### 1. Conversation Starters

- "How can I pray for you?"
- "God has helped me through so much…"
- "Have you ever considered faith or prayer?"

## 2. Acts of Kindness

Kindness softens the hardest hearts.

## 3. Share a Scripture

One verse can change a life.

## 4. Share Christian Content

Songs, sermons, or encouragements online.

## 5. Live in a Way That Honors God

Your lifestyle is a silent witness.

**6. Be Ready**

Carry a tract, Scripture card, or simple note of encouragement.


Witnessing is not an event — it is a lifestyle.

## VII. Leading Someone to Christ (A Simple Guide)

Many believers freeze when someone says: "I want to be saved."

But leading a soul to Christ is simple.

**Guide them to:**

**1. Acknowledge their need**

"We have all sinned…"

**2. Believe in Jesus**

"That Christ died for our sins…"

### 3. Confess Him as Lord

"Jesus, come into my heart. I receive You."

### 4. Pray With Them

Lead them gently in a sincere prayer of repentance and faith.

That moment is a miracle — heaven rejoices over one sinner who repents.

## VIII. Follow-Up: Helping New Believers Grow

Witnessing does not end when a person repeats the prayer.

**They must be:**

- placed in a church
- encouraged to read the Bible
- taught how to pray
- connected to a pastor or mentor
- supported as they grow

Winning a soul is the beginning.

Discipleship completes the mission.

## CLOSING CHARGE

Go into the world with confidence.

Share your story.

Share the gospel.

Let the Holy Ghost lead you.

God has placed people in your path who need hope, love, and truth.

Do not hide your light — let it shine.

Someone's eternity may change because you obeyed.

# REFLECTIVE SUMMARY

**In this chapter we learned:**

- Witnessing is every believer's responsibility.

- The gospel is simple and powerful.

- We can share our faith naturally and sincerely.

- The Holy Ghost empowers us to witness.

- Fear fades as we step out in obedience.

- Souls matter to God — and they must matter to us.

A witnessing believer is a fruitful believer.

## REFLECTIVE QUESTIONS

1. What keeps you from sharing your faith, and how can you overcome it?

2. Who in your life needs to hear about Jesus right now?

3. How can your personal testimony bless someone today?

4. What simple step can you take this week to witness intentionally?

5. How has the Holy Ghost helped you share your faith in the past?

## PRAYER

Father, in the name of Jesus,

Give me boldness to share the gospel.

Open my eyes to those around me who need You.

Use my words, my life, and my testimony for Your glory.

Fill me with the Holy Ghost and guide my steps.

Lead me to souls that are ready to receive.

Make me a faithful witness wherever I go.

**In Jesus' Name, Amen.**

# CHAPTER 12 — SERVING OTHERS: THE MINISTRY OF GODLY INFLUENCE

The Christian life is not meant to be lived in isolation.

As believers grow, God calls them to reach back and help others grow as well.

Every mature believer should be influencing someone.

Every growing believer should be guiding someone.

Every seasoned believer should be encouraging someone.

This is how the church becomes strong.

This is how faith passes from generation to generation.

This is how spiritual maturity multiplies.

Serving God is not only about what you do inside the church —it is about **how you touch and shape the lives of others.**

This chapter teaches believers how to serve others with humility, compassion, and influence — especially new believers who need guidance.

## I. What It Means to Serve Others

**Serving others is:**

- Helping

- Guiding

- Encouraging

- Strengthening

- Lifting

- Teaching

- Supporting

- and modeling Christlike living

It is not about authority or recognition.

It is about being an example, a helper, and a light.

**In the kingdom of God:**

Greatness is measured by how many people you serve, not how many serve you.

**Jesus Himself said:**

*"The Son of Man came not to be ministered unto, but to minister."*

If Jesus served, we must serve.

## II. Why Serving Others Is Essential to Spiritual Growth

A believer cannot grow to maturity without learning to serve others.

**Serving others:**

- deepens humility

- strengthens love

- develops patience

- increases compassion

- builds responsibility

- stabilizes spiritual maturity

- reflects Christ's character

God grows us so we can bless others.

And as we bless others, God grows us even more.

## III. The Power of Godly Influence

**Influence simply means:**

Your life speaks so loudly that others want to follow your example.

You do not need a title to influence.

**You influence others by:**

- how you pray

- how you worship

- how you forgive

- how you endure trials

- how you love people

- how you walk in holiness

- how you handle conflict

- how you read and study the Bible

- how you treat others


People watch your life before they listen to your words.


Godly influence is one of the strongest forms of ministry.

## IV. "Follow Me as I Follow Christ" — The Pattern of Godly Influence

Paul gave us the clearest picture of Christian influence **when he said:**

*"Be ye followers of me, even as I also am of Christ."*

**— 1 Corinthians 11:1**

Paul was not lifting himself up.

**He was saying:**

- "Watch how I live."

- "Watch how I pray."

- "Watch how I endure trials."

- "Watch how I love people."

- "Watch how I obey Christ."

Then he invited believers to **imitate those same qualities**, because he himself was imitating Jesus.

**This teaches us:**

- We must live lives worth following.

- We must model spiritual maturity.

- We must demonstrate Christlike character.

- We must help new believers by our example.

- Influence is discipleship — and discipleship is influence.

Every believer should be able to say, with humility:

*"Follow me, as I follow Christ."*

This is spiritual reproduction.

This is how disciples are made.

This is how the church grows strong.

# V. Helping New Believers: The Ministry of Reproduction

One of the greatest responsibilities in the church is helping new believers grow.

**New believers need:**

- Examples
- Encouragement
- Accountability
- Patience
- instruction

- friendship

- someone to walk with them

Just as infants need care, so spiritual infants need guidance.

**Helping a new believer is not complicated. You simply:**

- share what God taught you

- walk with them through struggles

- show them how to pray

- help them understand Scripture

- encourage them to attend church

- model holiness

- strengthen them when they fall

- celebrate their progress

- correct gently and with love

This is **spiritual reproduction** —

replicating the work of Christ in someone else.

This is how churches grow strong.

This is how disciples multiply.

## VI. The Example Principle: You Reproduce Who You Are

People do not follow your words —

they follow your life.

If you are prayerful, you will produce prayerful believers.

If you are faithful, you will inspire faithfulness.

If you are kind, you will influence kindness.

If you are holy, others will desire holiness.

Your life becomes a pattern for others:

*"Be an example of the believers..."*

**(1 Timothy 4:12)**

Your character becomes a template.

Your commitment becomes a standard.

Your walk becomes a light.

This is spiritual leadership without a title.

## VII. How to Serve Others Effectively

Here are simple, practical ways to **influence and strengthen others:**

### 1. Be Available

People grow when someone makes time for them.

### 2. Be Encouraging

A kind word can save someone from giving up.

### 3. Be Patient

New believers grow slowly — just as you did.

## 4. Be Prayerful

Praying for someone is the greatest act of service.

## 5. Be a Listener

Sometimes people need understanding more than advice.

## 6. Be Honest

Speak truth in love, not harshness.

## 7. Be Consistent

Your steadiness becomes their anchor.

Serving is not about perfection —

it is about presence.

## VIII. Serving Without a Position

Not everyone will carry a title.

But everyone carries responsibility.

**You can serve:**

- in your home
- on your job
- among friends
- at church
- online
- in private conversations

- in public witness

- through kindness

- through prayer

Serving God is simply serving people in His name.

## IX. The Blessings of Serving Others

When you serve others, **God blesses you:**

- your joy increases

- your faith deepens

- your purpose becomes clearer

- your maturity grows

- your influence expands

- your walk becomes stronger

- your heart becomes softer

Serving others is one of the greatest ways to grow spiritually.

God rewards those who serve with humility.

## CLOSING CHARGE

Serve someone.

Strengthen someone.

Encourage someone.

Lift someone.

Walk alongside a new believer and help them grow.

Let your life be a pattern worth imitating.

Be the example God has called you to be.

You reproduce who you are —

so walk in a way that others can safely follow.

# REFLECTIVE SUMMARY

In this chapter **we learned:**

- Serving others is a calling for every believer.

- Influence is one of the most powerful ministries.

- New believers need guidance, patience, and examples.

- Paul taught us to lead by imitation, not by title.

- You reproduce what God has developed in you.

- Serving without a title is still ministry.

- God rewards those who serve faithfully.

Serving others is how we extend the love of Christ.

# REFLECTIVE QUESTIONS

1. Who has God placed in your life for you to influence spiritually?

2. What example does your life provide for others to follow?

3. How can you better serve and support new believers?

4. What qualities do you want God to develop in you so you can reproduce them in others?

5. What step can you take this week to intentionally serve someone in love?

## PRAYER

Father, in the name of Jesus,

Teach me to serve others with humility and compassion.

Make my life an example that reflects Your love.

Give me the wisdom to guide new believers and help them grow.

Use my words, my actions, and my character to influence others for Christ.

Help me reproduce spiritual strength in those around me.

Let my life bring glory to Your name.

**In Jesus' Name, Amen.**

# CHAPTER 13 — HOW TO STUDY YOUR BIBLE: LEARNING TO FEED YOURSELF SPIRITUALLY

One of the most important steps in growing as a believer is learning how to study the Bible for yourself.

Hearing the Word preached is necessary.

Attending Bible study is important.

But spiritual growth becomes strong and steady when you learn how to sit with God's Word and allow the Holy Spirit to teach you directly.

Studying the Bible is not only for pastors, teachers, or ministers.

It is for **every believer.**

God wants His people to understand His Word, apply it to their lives, and grow in wisdom and faith.

This chapter gives you a simple, step-by-step guide to studying the Bible in a way that is clear, enjoyable, and spiritually fruitful.

## I. Why Bible Study Is Essential

Reading the Bible brings blessing.

Studying the Bible brings understanding, direction, and strength.

**Here's why Bible study matters:**

### 1. It feeds your spirit.

Just as the body needs food, the soul needs Scripture.

### 2. It renews your mind.

Bible study transforms your thinking and corrects wrong ideas.

### 3. It builds your faith.

"Faith comes by hearing… the Word of God."

### 4. It reveals God's will.

Scripture guides your decisions and choices.

### 5. It helps you resist temptation.

Jesus overcame the devil by quoting the Word.

### 6. It protects you from false teaching.

A believer who knows the Bible walks in truth and discernment.

Bible study strengthens everything in your spiritual life.

## II. Reading vs. Studying — Knowing the Difference

Many believers read the Bible, but few study it.

**There is a difference:**

**Reading**

Is moving through Scripture to become familiar with it.

It is good, necessary, and encouraging.

**Studying**

Is slowing down, asking questions, examining meaning, and applying the truth to your life.

**Reading** gives you an overview.

**Study** gives you understanding.

Both are needed — but studying takes you deeper.

## III. Preparing Your Heart Before You Study

Before you study the Bible, take a moment to prepare your heart.

### 1. Pray for understanding.

Ask the Holy Ghost to teach you.

He is the true Interpreter of Scripture.

### 2. Remove distractions.

Find a quiet place if possible.

**3. Have your tools ready.**

A Bible

A notebook or journal

A pen

(Optional) A dictionary or simple study guide

**4. Approach the Word with humility.**

Be ready to learn, change, and obey.

When your heart is prepared, the Word becomes alive.

## IV. A Simple Bible Study Method for All Believers

Here is a simple method that anyone — new believer or seasoned saint — **can use:**

**1. OBSERVATION** — What does the passage say?

Read the Scripture carefully.

**Ask:**

- Who is speaking?
- Who is being addressed?
- What is happening?
- What stands out?
- What repeated words or ideas do you see?

Do not jump to interpretation yet.

Just observe.

## 2. INTERPRETATION — What does it mean?

**Now ask:**

- What is the main point?

- What was God teaching in this passage?

- What does the context reveal?

- How would the original listeners have understood it?

- Is the Holy Ghost highlighting something to me?

Take your time.

Let Scripture explain Scripture.

## 3. APPLICATION — What should I do with what I learned?

The Bible was not written just to inform — but to transform. **Ask:**

- What is God calling me to do?

- What should change in my attitude, words, or actions?

- What promise should I believe?

- What sin should I confess?

- What step of obedience should I take?

Bible study becomes powerful when it leads to obedience.

## V. Easy Ways to Study Different Parts of the Bible

**Here are simple approaches to make your study effective:**

### 1. Verse-by-Verse Study

Choose a passage and study it slowly, one verse at a time.

Great for understanding depth.

### 2. Chapter Study

Read the whole chapter. Identify the main themes and ideas.

Great for structure and context.

## 3. Character Study

Study a person in the Bible — **Abraham, Joseph, Ruth, David, Paul, etc.**

Look at their strengths, weaknesses, and lessons.

Great for learning wisdom and life application.

## 4. Topical Study

Choose a topic such as:

- Faith
- Prayer
- Forgiveness
- Holiness
- the Holy Ghost

- spiritual warfare

Then find Scriptures on that topic.

Great for solving personal struggles or questions.

**5. Book Study**

Choose an entire book — such as **John, Ephesians**, or **Proverbs** — and read or study through it slowly.

Great for deeper understanding.

## VI. How to Let Scripture Shape Your Life

Studying the Bible becomes life-changing when **you allow it to:**

### 1. Correct your thinking

False beliefs cannot stand when the Word shines light.

### 2. Shape your behavior

The Bible transforms your habits, lifestyle, and decisions.

### 3. Strengthen your character

Daily study produces humility, wisdom, and discernment.

### 4. Guide your choices

God's Word becomes your compass.

### 5. Influence your relationships

Scripture teaches you how to treat people with love, patience, and grace.

Bible study must reach your heart — not just your head.

## VII. Practical Tips for Consistent Bible Study

**Here are simple ways to stay consistent:**

**1. Set a regular time**

Consistency is more important than length.

**2. Start with books that are easier to understand**

John, Mark, Psalms, Proverbs, James, Ephesians.

**3. Write down what you learn**

A Bible journal keeps your growth visible.

**4. Ask questions while reading**

Questions open the door to revelation.

**5. Memorize small portions**

Scripture hidden in the heart brings victory.

**6. Re-read passages**

Repetition brings deeper understanding.

**7. Let the Holy Ghost guide you**

He will lead you to the Scriptures you need for your season.

Bible study is a relationship, not an academic activity.

## VIII. The Role of the Holy Ghost in Bible Study

The Holy Ghost is the Teacher of the believer.

**He:**

- opens understanding

- reveals truth

- brings Scripture to remembrance

- convicts the heart

- comforts the soul

- gives revelation

- applies the Word personally

- protects from error

- shines light on hidden meaning

Without the Holy Ghost, Bible study becomes dry.

With Him, the Word becomes alive, powerful, and transformative.

Invite Him to teach you every time you open the Bible.

## CLOSING CHARGE

Study the Word with purpose.

Do not rush.

Do not skip.

Let the Scriptures speak to your heart.

Take time to listen to what the Holy Ghost is saying.

The more you study the Bible, the stronger you will become.

The more you understand the Bible, the more clearly you will hear God's voice.

Let His Word be your daily bread — your guide, your strength, and your anchor.

# REFLECTIVE SUMMARY

**In this chapter we learned:**

- Studying the Bible is essential for spiritual maturity.

- Reading is different from studying — both are needed.

- The heart must be prepared before study.

- A simple method — Observation, Interpretation, Application — works for all believers.

- There are many helpful ways to study different parts of Scripture.

- The Holy Ghost is the believer's Teacher.

- Consistency in study produces strong, wise, mature Christians.

The Bible is God speaking to you — study it with reverence and expectation.

# REFLECTIVE QUESTIONS

1. What hinders you most from studying the Bible regularly?

2. Which Bible study method do you feel most comfortable with right now?

3. How has the Holy Ghost helped you understand Scripture in the past?

4. What book of the Bible do you want to study next, and why?

5. How can you apply what you learned today to your daily study?

## PRAYER

Father, in the name of Jesus,

Give me a hunger for Your Word.

Teach me how to study with understanding and purpose.

Open my eyes to see truth, and open my heart to receive it.

Holy Ghost, be my Teacher and Guide.

Help me apply the Scriptures to my life so that I may grow in wisdom and maturity.

Let Your Word transform every part of me.

**In Jesus' Name, Amen.**

## CHAPTER 14 — A COURSE FOR READING THROUGH THE BIBLE IN ONE YEAR

One of the most rewarding commitments a believer can make is the decision to read through the entire Bible.

For many Christians, this becomes a turning point in their spiritual growth— a year when the Scriptures come alive, their understanding deepens, and their relationship with God grows stronger and more mature.

Yet many are intimidated by the thought of reading the whole Bible.

Some start with excitement but soon become overwhelmed. Others feel unsure where to begin or how to stay consistent.

This chapter is designed to give you a **simple, manageable, and encouraging plan** to help you read through the Bible in one year.

The purpose is not to rush, but to **walk with God, day by day,** allowing the Holy Ghost to open your understanding as you journey through the Scriptures.

This is a gentle, flexible guide—a plan that works for new believers and seasoned saints alike.

## I. Why Read Through the Entire Bible?

Reading through the Bible from Genesis to Revelation builds spiritual maturity. It gives you a foundation that cannot come from sermons alone or from scattered devotional reading.

**Here are several reasons this journey matters:**

**1. You see the whole story of redemption.**

Creation, fall, covenant, prophecy, the coming of Christ, the birth of the Church, and the final victory.

**2. You understand God's character.**

You see His mercy, justice, holiness, patience, and faithfulness throughout generations.

**3. You learn how Scripture connects.**

The Old Testament prepares the way for the New.

The New Testament fulfills what the Old foretold.

**4. Your faith grows.**

Daily exposure to God's Word strengthens your mind and spirit.

**5. You become rooted and grounded.**

A believer who knows the Bible is difficult to mislead or shaken.

Reading through the Bible isn't just informational—it is transformational.

## II. A Simple, Doable Approach

Many reading plans fail because they are too complicated or too demanding. But spiritual growth thrives with **simplicity.**

**Your reading plan should be:**

- Clear
- Gentle
- Balanced
- Flexible
- Achievable
- Spirit-led

This chapter gives you a monthly outline, not a daily checklist.

This keeps the plan light, freeing, and spiritually refreshing.

If you fall behind, you do not feel defeated—

you simply continue the journey.

## III. A Monthly Course for Reading Through the Bible

Below is a **twelve-month guide** to help you read the entire Bible at a comfortable pace.

You can follow it strictly, or you can stretch it into 15–18 months if needed.

The goal is not speed—

the goal is **steady growth.**

Each month contains a portion of the Old Testament, a portion of the New Testament, and an optional Psalm or Proverb emphasis.

**MONTH 1** — Genesis & Matthew

The beginnings of creation and the beginnings of the gospel story.

**MONTH 2** — Exodus & Mark

God delivers His people; Jesus ministers with power.

**MONTH 3** — Leviticus, Numbers & Luke

Holiness, order, and the compassionate ministry of Christ.

**MONTH 4** — Deuteronomy & John

A renewed covenant and a deeper revelation of Jesus.

**MONTH 5** — Joshua, Judges, Ruth & Acts

Conquest, cycles of disobedience, redemption, and the birth of the Church.

**MONTH 6** — 1 & 2 Samuel; 1 & 2 Corinthians

Leadership, kingship, and Paul's instruction to the church.

**MONTH 7** — 1 & 2 Kings; Galatians; Ephesians; Philippians; Colossians

History of Israel's kings and key teachings for Christian living.

**MONTH 8** — 1 & 2 Chronicles; Thessalonians; Timothy; Titus

A retelling of Israel's history and practical New Testament counsel.

**MONTH 9** — Ezra, Nehemiah, Esther; Romans

Restoration and the foundational doctrines of the Christian faith.

**MONTH 10** — Job; Psalms; Proverbs

Wisdom, worship, and life lessons.

**MONTH 11** — Isaiah; Jeremiah; Lamentations

Major prophetic messages calling Israel back to God.

**MONTH 12** — Ezekiel; Daniel; Minor Prophets; Hebrews through Revelation

Prophetic revelation and the final fulfillment of God's plan.

## IV. A Gentle Weekly Rhythm

To keep the plan manageable, **use this weekly structure:**

### Read 5 days per week

Give yourself two rest or catch-up days.

### Read 2–3 chapters per day

Enough to move forward, not enough to overwhelm.

### Use Sundays for reflection

Meditate on what you read instead of rushing.

This rhythm encourages consistency instead of pressure.

## V. Tips for Staying Encouraged

### 1. Pray before you read.

Ask the Holy Ghost to open your understanding.

### 2. Choose a consistent time.

Morning, lunch break, or evening—whatever works.

### 3. Keep a simple journal.

Write down insights, questions, or memorable verses.

### 4. Don't get stuck in difficult sections.

Keep reading; clarity often comes later.

**5. If you fall behind, don't quit.**

Pick up where you left off and continue forward.

**6. Celebrate milestones.**

Finishing a book of the Bible is an accomplishment.

Consistency—not perfection—is the goal.

## VI. The Blessing of Completing the Journey

By the end of the year—or whenever your journey concludes—**you will discover:**

- A stronger understanding of Scripture
- A deeper prayer life
- Clearer spiritual discernment
- More confidence in your walk with God
- Greater maturity and stability
- An increased sensitivity to the Holy Ghost

Reading through the Bible builds a foundation for lifelong spiritual growth.

## CLOSING CHARGE

Commit yourself to the journey.

Start with expectation, not fear.

The Holy Ghost is your Teacher,

and God's Word is your daily bread.

Walk slowly.

Walk consistently.

Walk prayerfully.

And may the Scriptures shape your faith, strengthen your heart, and draw you closer to the Lord each day.

# REFLECTIVE SUMMARY

**In this chapter we learned:**

- Why reading the entire Bible is essential
- How a simple plan encourages growth
- A monthly course to guide your journey
- A weekly rhythm to keep you consistent
- Practical tips for staying encouraged
- The spiritual blessings of finishing the course

The Word of God is a treasure—this plan helps you uncover it.

# REFLECTIVE QUESTIONS

1. What challenges have hindered your Bible reading in the past?

2. Which month of the plan seems most exciting to you?

3. How can you create a routine to support daily reading?

4. What do you hope God will show you through this journey?

5. Who could you encourage to join you in reading through the Bible?

## PRAYER

Father, in the name of Jesus,

Give me a steady heart to read Your Word with faith and expectation.

Open my understanding as I walk through the Scriptures.

Let the Holy Ghost teach me, strengthen me, and guide me.

May this journey draw me closer to You, deepen my faith, and renew my mind.

Help me finish the course with joy, wisdom, and spiritual maturity.

**In Jesus' Name, Amen.**

# CONCLUSION

As you come to the close of this book, remember that growing in the faith is not a one-time event but a lifelong journey. The truths you have learned—about salvation, the foundations of Christian doctrine, the nature of God, worship, prayer, spiritual growth, church fellowship, and personal holiness—are meant to shape the way you live every day.

The Christian life is simple, but it is not shallow. God calls us to walk with Him in humility, obedience, and trust. He invites us to study His Word, surrender our will, and follow the leading of the Holy Ghost. And He strengthens us through fellowship with the body of Christ, the Church.

Whether you are a new believer taking your first steps or a seasoned saint renewing your foundation, remember this:

Your spiritual growth matters. Your faith matters. Your walk with God matters.

Do not be discouraged by slow progress.

Do not compare yourself with others.

Do not lose heart in trials.

Keep your eyes on Jesus.

Stay anchored in the Scriptures.

Remain faithful in prayer and worship.

Walk in love, humility, and obedience.

The same God who saved you will also sustain you. He will finish the work He began in you, and He will strengthen you to stand before Him with joy.

May this book serve as a steady guide as you grow in grace, deepen your understanding, and walk boldly in the truth of God's Word. My prayer is that the Holy Ghost will continue to teach you, lead you, correct you, comfort you, and empower you to live a life that brings glory to God.

Keep growing.

Keep learning.

Keep walking with God.

The best days of your spiritual journey are still ahead.

# ACKNOWLEDGMENTS

First and foremost, I give all glory, honor, and praise to God through our Lord and Savior Jesus Christ. Without His mercy, grace, and calling, this book would not exist. Every page is a testament to His faithfulness and the transforming power of the Holy Ghost.

I gratefully acknowledge the spiritual heritage of the Church Of God In Christ, founded by **Bishop Charles Harrison Mason.** His unwavering commitment to holiness, prayer, and sound doctrine has shaped generations of believers—including myself. His legacy continues to inspire my ministry, my teaching, and my pursuit of a life wholly led by the Spirit.

I extend heartfelt appreciation to the pastors, teachers, and spiritual leaders who poured into my life and encouraged me to remain faithful to the Word of God. I am especially grateful for the late **Dr. Gwendolyn McCurry,** whose prayers, counsel, and prophetic ministry were instrumental during some of the most challenging seasons of my journey. Her obedience to God left an imprint that continues to guide, strengthen, and steady me today.

I also express sincere gratitude to **Pastor James H. Bannerman** for his steadfast leadership and example of servant ministry. His influence helped shape my understanding of humility, discipline, and spiritual responsibility in the life of a believer.

My appreciation extends to **Pastor Kennedy G. Lockhart,** his wife, and the entire Church – Church Of God In Christ family, whose kindness, support, and receptiveness to the ministry God placed in me have been a continual source of encouragement. Their love and fellowship have reminded me that ministry is not carried alone, but within a community that uplifts and strengthens one another in Christ.

To every saint, friend, and believer who has prayed for me, encouraged me, or stood with me along the way—thank you. Your faith, your hunger for truth, and your love for God's Word inspire me to write, teach, and serve with renewed passion and commitment. May the Lord reward your faithfulness, enrich your walk with Him, and continue to bless you in every good work.

## ABOUT THE AUTHOR

Eld Joel Latimore Jr. is an ordained pastor, teacher, preacher, and prolific author whose ministry spans decades of faithful service to God's people. A man shaped by prayer, discipline, and the fire of the Holy Ghost, Elder Latimore writes with a unique blend of authority, compassion, and prophetic clarity for the edification of the body of Christ.

His books reflect deep biblical insight, spiritual maturity, and practical wisdom, all grounded in an unwavering commitment to holiness and personal accountability. With a pastor's heart and a watchman's eye, he calls believers back to the foundations of the Christian life—prayer, consecration, early rising, daily devotion, and complete dependence on the Holy Ghost.

A proud U.S. Army veteran, Elder Latimore carries both the discipline of a soldier and the sensitivity of a servant of God. His personal testimony of transformation, deliverance, and the guiding work of the Holy Ghost has inspired countless believers to pursue a deeper walk with the Lord.

Through preaching, teaching, mentorship, and writing, he strives to strengthen the church, build strong families, restore hope, and awaken the next generation to their God-given identity and purpose. His ministry is marked by humility, integrity, and a burning desire to see Christ formed in the hearts of men and women everywhere.

Elder Latimore's life message can be summarized in these simple but powerful words:

***"Walk with God daily — and He will make your steps sure."***

www.ingramcontent.com/pod-product-compliance
Lightning Source LLC
Chambersburg PA
CBHW080410170426
43194CB00015B/2765